TRAVELS IN HAWAII

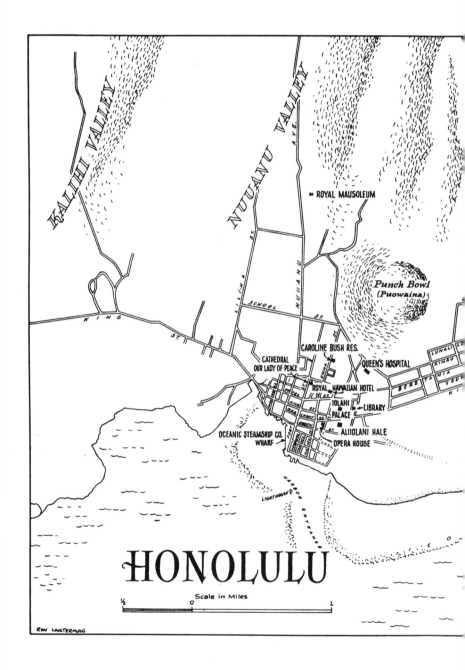

KALIHI VALLEY

NUUANU VALLEY

NUUANU AVE.

● ROYAL MAUSOLEUM

Punch Bowl
(Puowaina)

LILIHA ST.

SCHOOL ST.

NUUANU ST.

BERETANIA ST.

KING ST.

CAROLINE BUSH RES.

CATHEDRAL
OUR LADY OF PEACE

QUEEN'S HOSPITAL

LUNALILO

KINAU

BERETANIA

PIIKOI

YOUNG

KING ST.

ROYAL HAWAIIAN HOTEL

NUUANU ST.

FORT ST.

IOLANI
PALACE

LIBRARY

ALIIOLANI HALE

OCEANIC STEAMSHIP CO.
WHARF

GREEN ST.

OPERA HOUSE

LIGHTHOUSE

HARBOR ENTRANCE

HONOLULU

Scale in Miles

½   0   1

RAY LANTERMAN

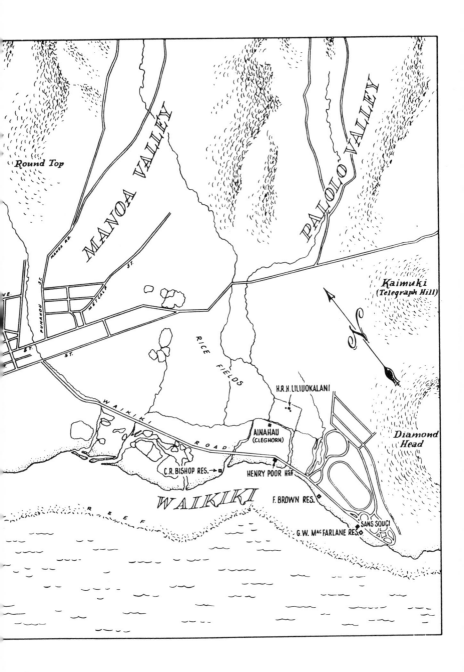

Round Top

MANOA VALLEY

PALOLO VALLEY

MANOA RD.

ALEXANDER ST.

METCALF ST.

AVE. ST.

DILLINGHAM ST.

PUNAHOU ST.

B. ST.

ST.

RICE FIELDS

Kaimuki
(Telegraph Hill)

N

WAIKIKI

H.R.H. LILIUOKALANI

AINAHAU
(CLEGHORN)

ROAD

Diamond
Head

C.R. BISHOP RES.

HENRY POOR HSE.

F. BROWN RES.

WAIKIKI

G.W. MacFARLANE RES.

SANS SOUCI

REEF

TRAVELS IN
HAWAII

ROBERT LOUIS STEVENSON

EDITED AND WITH AN INTRODUCTION
BY A. GROVE DAY

UNIVERSITY OF HAWAII PRESS
HONOLULU

Library of Congress Cataloging-in-Publication Data
Stevenson, Robert Louis, 1850-1904.
Travels in Hawaii / Robert Louis Stevenson;
edited and with an introduction by A. Grove Day.
p. cm.
Reprint. Originally published: Honolulu:
University Press of Hawaii, c1973.
Includes bibliographical references.
ISBN 0-8248-1397-9
1. Hawaii — Description and travel — To 1950.
2. Stevenson, Robert Louis, 1850-1904 —
Homes and haunts — Hawaii. I. Day, A. Grove
(Arthur Grove), 1904-   . II. Title.
DU623.S84   1991
919.6904'4 — DC20   91-2351
CIP

Book design by Roger J. Eggers
Cover photo: Stevenson with King Kalākaua.
Courtesy Hawaii State Archives.

University of Hawaii Press books are printed on
acid-free paper and meet the guidelines for permanence
and durability of the Council on Library Resources

CONTENTS

CONTENTS

PREFACE

Many people who have enjoyed the books of world-famed Robert Louis Stevenson, such as *Kidnapped, Treasure Island,* and *The Strange Case of Dr. Jekyll and Mr. Hyde,* are not aware that their author spent the last six years of his life in the South Seas and wrote several fine volumes about his adventures among the Pacific islands.

The lifelong search for health by this frail genius led him to cruise with his family among the warm isles of the South Pacific in his chartered yacht *Casco.* He arrived in Hawaii in 1889, during the reign of the last king of the archipelago. For five months, Robert Louis Stevenson—known around the world as R.L.S.—wrote, traveled, and enjoyed the hospitality of the people of the "eight islands," ranging from the royal family to the lone schoolmaster of a Kona Coast village. Stevenson chatted with the half-Scottish, half-Hawaiian Princess Ka'iulani beneath her father's banyan tree at Waikiki, and wrote for her a poem treasured by residents and visitors alike. Stevenson returned to these islands in 1893 for a five-week visit, and found there a very different political climate. Pro-American annexationists had

PREFACE

overthrown his friend Queen Liliʻuokalani and proclaimed the right to set up a Republic of Hawaii that eventually was to lead to the establishment of America's fiftieth state.

Stevenson's writings about Hawaii are more considerable than most readers would expect. These writings, for several reasons, have not been widely circulated. The chapters he wrote about his adventures at Kona and the City of Refuge and on the island of Molokai were omitted from most editions of his collected works. The lively letters that he and his wife sent to friends reflect their enthusiasm for the Hawaiian scene. The scathing "Letter to the Reverend Dr. Hyde," in which R.L.S. tried to defend Father Damien de Veuster—"martyr of Molokai," whose effigy today stands in Statuary Hall in Washington, D.C.—is a classic of invective based on Stevenson's visit to the isolation station on the island of Molokai. Two of Stevenson's best short stories—"The Bottle Imp" and "The Isle of Voices" —have settings in Hawaii. Six poems written in the islands have here been rescued from near oblivion. Stevenson's journal of travel on the Kona Coast has been transcribed and is here published for the first time. Photographs showing the variegated moods of the Stevenson party during the days of King Kalākaua, the Merry Monarch, appear in the clothbound edition. All these records of a romantic interlude in the life of a cherished master of the English language are illuminated by a factual essay by the editor, which tries to reject the legends that have grown up about Stevenson and Hawaii, and to determine what the Scottish author and his friends

PREFACE

actually achieved during their days of roving in a vanished kingdom.

The convenience of the modern reader has been considered in making the text (with the exception of the journal, which is printed verbatim) conform to modern practice in spelling, punctuation, capitalization, and the use of quotation marks and italics. *Webster's Third New International Dictionary* and *Webster's Geographical Dictionary* have been supplemented by the *Hawaiian-English Dictionary* of Mary K. Pukui and Samuel H. Elbert. The hamza or inverted apostrophe is used in Hawaiian words to indicate a glottal stop. Editorial comments are enclosed in brackets. Omission of passages in the letters which do not bear upon Hawaii is always indicated by ellipses.

Editing the words of an author I have read with pleasure since first I learned to read has been a humbling task. It has been lightened by a lengthy professional concern with the fascinating literature in English about the Hawaiian and other Pacific islands, and by a residence of more than a quarter of a century in Hawaii. My chief debt is to my friend and former student, Sister Martha Mary McGaw, C.S.J., whose fine book, *Stevenson in Hawaii,* was published in 1950, during the period of my chairmanship of the Department of English at the University of Hawaii. Her volume, now unfortunately out of print, contains an excellent bibliography on the subject. Out of the many sources available, I have depended most upon J. C. Furnas' *Voyage to Windward* (New York: William Sloane Associates, 1951) and Arthur Johnstone's *Recollections of Rob-*

PREFACE

ert Louis Stevenson in the Pacific (London: Chatto & Windus, 1905). The transcript of the "Journal of a Visit to the Kona Coast" (Manuscript HM 2412), is reproduced by the kind permission of the Huntington Library, San Marino, California.

A. GROVE DAY
Senior Professor of
English, Emeritus
University of Hawaii

INTRODUCTION

ROBERT LOUIS STEVENSON
AND HAWAII

The foreign author most beloved by the people of Hawaii first came to the islands in 1889.

The graceful yacht *Casco,* with Robert Louis Balfour Stevenson and his family aboard, had left Tahiti on Christmas Day, 1888, on a "most disastrous" passage, with "calms, squalls, head sea, waterspouts of rain, hurricane weather all about." [1] After almost a month, the vessel sighted the "Big Island" of Hawaii. A fair, strong wind blew, and the *Casco,* carrying jib, foresail, and mainsail—all single-reefed—flew along with her lee rail under. A heavy swell, the highest that Stevenson had ever seen, came tearing after them about a point and a half off the wind, but fortunately never crashed once upon the hull of the speeding *Casco.*

The wind then died down, and for two days the anxious passengers lay becalmed off the Kona Coast

NOTE: All the editor's notes for this introduction are numbered and appear at the end of this section.

while their food supply, except for salt beef and biscuit, gave out. When the wind did come, it swept them past the islands of Maui and Molokai and into Honolulu Harbor at an alarming speed. Stevenson got his first view of the city, with its busy wharfs, low buildings, and background of swelling green mountains. At three o'clock on the afternoon of Friday, January 24, 1889, the *Casco* anchored. Even here, in mid-Pacific, reporters came out to interview the celebrated visitor, whose vessel had been so long overdue that it had been given up for lost.

Robert Louis Stevenson was then at the height of his popularity. Born in Edinburgh in 1850, he had forsaken the family calling of lighthouse engineer to take a law degree, and then had found his true career in literature. Publication of books like *Treasure Island, The Strange Case of Doctor Jekyll and Mr. Hyde,* and *Kidnapped* had brought him renown, and his industry with the pen had brought him a decent income as well. After broad travels, mainly in search of health—he had been frail in childhood and suffered all his life from tuberculosis—he had embarked on the romantic cruise that was to lead him to spend his final years among the Pacific islands.

S. S. McClure, head of a publishing syndicate, offered Stevenson a substantial sum if, during a proposed voyage for his health, he would write a series of travel sketches. Stevenson had wanted to cruise through the South Seas ever since his lonely stay in San Francisco late in 1879, when he had met Charles Warren Stoddard, writer of sketches and poems, in the "eyrie" on Rincon Hill. Stoddard, who along with Herman Melville was termed by R.L.S. as one of the two writers, both Americans, who had "touched the South Seas with any genius," [2] had made four trips to the Pacific islands, and his tales of Tahiti, Honolulu, and Molokai had aroused Stevenson's romantic yearning to range the latitudes of the noble brown races. Surely a proper yacht could be found that would carry the author and his family to the isles of summer!

The *Casco* was chartered from her multimillionaire owner, Dr. Samuel Merritt of Oakland, California, who was reluctant to entrust his jewel to anyone—especially to the slight Bohemian character who, at their first meeting, impressed the doctor as verging on insanity. Stevenson's bank account, fattened by a legacy from his father and an advance from McClure, prevailed. The charter gave Merritt the right to name as captain his old friend Albert H. Otis, who likewise was dubious. Stevenson looked to him much more aged than his thirty-nine years. R.L.S. was a stumbling skeleton, with a grotesquely gay air. Yet everyone was struck by his glowing brown eyes, which all his life had defied the hovering specter of death. Had Captain Otis been a literary man—which he was not—he might have recalled the description of R.L.S. in the sonnet by William Ernest Henley:

> . . . Valiant in velvet, light in ragged luck,
> Most vain, most generous, sternly critical,
> Buffoon and poet, lover and sensualist;
> A deal of Ariel, just a streak of Puck,
> Much Antony, of Hamlet most of all,
> And something of the Shorter-Catechist.

INTRODUCTION

Before the voyage was over, captain and charterer were to learn to respect each other's mettle.

The *Casco* was a two-masted schooner with clean lines and spotless decks. Dr. Merritt had designed her to be one of the finest yachts afloat, with her cabin lined with mirrors and her salon chairs cushioned with velvet. Her graceful strength was to be tested to the limit in the forthcoming cruise on the ocean that is not always pacific. She glided through the Golden Gate on the afternoon of June 28, 1888; and Robert Louis Stevenson gazed for the last time on the American continent. The islands were to claim him for their own, and the Pacific would give him rich material to add splendor to the works of his final years.

Accompanying "Louis"—as he was always called in the family—was an oddly assorted group of relatives. Most essential to his survival was his wife, Frances (Fanny) Matilda Van de Grift Osbourne, a divorcée with two children. Eleven years his elder, Fanny, reared in a rough Indiana town, had met him at an artists' colony near Paris when he was twenty-six, and they had fallen romantically in love. Stevenson had made his first trip to San Francisco, in fact, to help Fanny through the dangerous strain of divorce proceedings, and had himself become an invalid. They were married in that city on May 19, 1880, and then for eight years had seldom been separated.

Fanny's son—(Samuel) Lloyd Osbourne, born in 1868—was also aboard, a gawky, bespectacled fellow just reaching his majority and dreaming of a writer's career. Stevenson's widowed mother, accompanied by a maid named Valentine Roch, was likewise enjoying the cruise. Mrs. Thomas Stevenson, born Margaret Isabella Balfour and usually called Maggie, dressed as primly as Queen Victoria and wore similar starched widow's caps. She and the other ladies stood the rigors of the sea remarkably well.

Stevenson's first Pacific island, touching "a virginity of sense," [3] was Nuku Hiva in the Marquesas, scene of Melville's *Typee,* a book that Louis had carried away after a visit to Stoddard's San Francisco studio. For six happy months the party were guests of the people of the Marquesas. Then, threading the low atolls of the Tuamotu or Dangerous Archipelago, the *Casco* took the voyagers to the famed pearl fisheries. In September, although his health had seemingly improved, Louis was stricken with a lung ailment and the *Casco* headed for Papeete, capital of French Oceania. Recovered, the author obtained much valuable information about Tahiti before embarking on the long traverse to Hawaii.

Off Honolulu, Fanny's daughter Isobel, called "Belle," born in 1858, came out to the yacht with her husband, Joseph Dwight Strong, an artist who had come to Hawaii to paint for the royal court. At once the Stevensons were taken into the "royal crowd," the gay stratum of society that clustered around the palace built for His Hawaiian Majesty, David Kalākaua.

King Kalākaua and his consort, Kapi'olani, had been on the throne since he won a stormy election in 1874. His attempts to restore personal rule to the monarchy were to end in its destruction, but while it lasted he was always the leading actor in a reign that sometimes resembled a Viennese operetta. The king could speak and write well both in Hawaiian and English. His court was a center of music and culture; he had composed the words to "Hawai'i Pono'i," the national anthem, and his name appeared as author of *Legends and Myths of Hawaii,* edited by R. M. Daggett, the first important book in English to deal with the old tales. Of Kalākaua, Stevenson's friend Stoddard wrote: "Oh, what a king was he! Such a king as one reads of in nursery tales. He was all things to all men, a most companionable person. Possessed of rare refinement, he was as much at ease with a crew of 'rollicking rams' as in the throne room." [4] The first telephone to be installed on the capital island of Oahu was strung between Iolani Palace and the Royal Boathouse, setting for many a hilarious evening amid hula girls and poker tables.

The king had won popularity by obtaining a long-desired reciprocity treaty which allowed sugar from Hawaii to enter the United States free of duty. He had toured the United States in 1874–1875, the first monarch ever to do so. He had toured the world in 1881, again setting a royal precedent. On his travels he had seen the crown jewels of several nations and, in 1883, on the ninth anniversary of his election, Kalākaua personally crowned himself and his queen within the bandstand in the palace grounds, before a crowd of eight thousand of his subjects.

The king's fatal temptation to follow the advice of self-seeking adventurers like Celso Caesar Moreno and Walter Murray Gibson lost him much popular-

ity and aroused strong reform movements. Spurred
on by Gibson, Kalākaua decided to make himself
the primate of a Polynesian League comprising all
the islands of the Pacific that had not been taken over
by one or another European power. He sent a delegation led by John Edward Bush to Samoa, where
Bush signed an agreement of confederation with
Chief Malietoa. To back up this interference in
Samoan affairs, among the islands where Germany,
Britain, and the United States were fighting a three-
way battle for dominance, Kalākaua sent his "navy"
—a refitted guano carrier named *Kaimiloa,* with a
drunken captain and a crew mainly of boys released
from the Honolulu reform school. The collapse of
this grandiose adventure, aggravated by scandal and
corruption at court, led to Gibson's ejection from
the islands and the forced signing by Kalākaua of a
more liberal constitution—the "Bayonet Constitution," as it was termed by his strong-willed sister
Lili'uokalani. Resentful, the king hung on to whatever powers remained—mainly a legislative veto—
and continued to earn his sobriquet of the "Merry
Monarch."

Joe and Belle Strong had lived in Honolulu for
more than six years with their son Austin, who was
eight years old at the time of the Stevensons' visit
and who was later to become a noted American play-
wright. Belle had run secret errands between the
king and Gibson and had designed the Royal Order
of the Star of Oceania. Joe had been the official artist
with the ill-omened delegation to Samoa. Both were
leading residents of Honolulu, which Stevenson once
ironically described as a modern town "brisk with

traffic, and the palace with its guards, and the great hotel, and Mr. Berger's band with their uniforms and outlandish instruments." [5] On the first night ashore, the *Casco* party were guests of the Strongs at the sprawling "great hotel," the Royal Hawaiian, then situated at Hotel and Richards streets. Other residents came to the dining table to meet the Stevensons and Captain Otis, and to listen to the lively yarns of R.L.S. concerning the voyage and South Sea life. The cruel waves and short rations were forgotten over roast beef and wine.

That night and for several nights the Stevensons lodged at 40 Emma Street, home of Mrs. Caroline Bush, a woman of social prestige. Since the Strong family also resided there, it became evident that the Stevensons needed a place of their own—especially a place where Louis could continue his writing in some solitude. Henry Poor, son of Mrs. Bush, had been secretary to the embassy to Samoa, where he had become friendly with Joe Strong. Poor's mother suggested that Henry let the visitors have his Waikiki bungalow called Manuia Lanai, on the beach at the spot still known as Sans Souci. (A towering apartment house rises there nowadays, flanked by other high-rise buildings for wealthy residents.)

Two days after the *Casco* anchored, Stevenson and Lloyd Osbourne were formally presented to King Kalākaua at Iolani Palace. Letters of introduction obtained in California were unnecessary, for the king knew of Stevenson's fame as a storyteller, and soon the royal dignity and affability charmed the Scottish wanderer, who had inherited a respect for sovereignty and had acquired an admiration for Polynesians.

A few days later the king returned the call, in the cabin of the *Casco*. R.L.S. read his ballad "Ticonderoga." Captain Otis played the accordion, Belle Strong danced, and Lloyd Osbourne sang "The Fine Pacific Islands." After this gay party Louis was firmly bound to the royalist cause. He was, however, astounded by Kalākaua's drinking capacity. The champagne bottles came and went—five of them, along with two bottles of brandy. Yet, when the king rose to depart, he was "perceptibly more dignified," nothing more.[6] Louis was blissfully unaware that Kalākaua continued his day of celebration by dining aboard a visiting warship and winning the applause of her officers in a drinking sweepstakes.

Kalākaua and Princess Liliʻuokalani were the special guests at a luau given by Henry Poor at Manuia Lanai on Sunday, February 3. The feast offered the traditional menu—chicken, pig, poi, raw fish, a type of seaweed called limu, roasted kukui nuts, and baked dog—a favorite dish with the king. The high point of the evening was the presentation by Fanny to Kalākaua of a golden pearl from the Tuamotus. Stevenson read aloud his graceful sonnet offering "the ocean jewel to the island king." It was on this occasion that Arthur Richardson went about taking photographs of the luau. He focused his camera on the king and R.L.S. sitting gravely in conversation. Later he went to an opening in the lattice of the lanai and snapped the famous picture of Liliʻuokalani facing Stevenson with regal composure.

INTRODUCTION

The next evening the *Hale Naua* ("House of Ancient Science") held its annual meeting at Iolani Palace. According to the charter of this secret society, which combined aspects of Masonry with the rites of pagan chiefs, it had been organized forty quadrillions of years after the foundation of the world. One historian believed it was intended "partly as an agency for the revival of heathenism, partly to pander to vice, and indirectly to serve as a political machine." [7] The Strongs and Stevensons, with the exception of Louis himself, were in attendance. On this open occasion it is probable that *'ume,* the favorite game of the members, was omitted. In this game the companion of an evening's pleasure was chosen by rolling a ball of twine in the direction of the desired lady. The game has been termed something like Post Office, but more serious.

South Sea voyaging had put Louis into as good health as he could ever expect to enjoy. The warm airs of Hawaii and sea bathing at Waikiki had brought him to something like normal spirits, and enabled him to meet his literary obligations. One can appreciate his unusual vivacity as well as his usual industry by anticipating a letter he was to write in 1893 to George Meredith: "For fourteen years I have not had a day's real health; I have wakened sick and gone to bed weary; and I have done my work unflinchingly. I have written in bed, and written out of it, written in hemorrhages, written in sickness, written torn by coughing, written when my head swam for weakness." [8]

Now Stevenson was buried in literary labors. He was desperately trying to finish his novel *The Master of Ballantrae.* With foolhardy courage he had allowed the editor of *Scribner's Magazine* to embark on serial publication without himself having any clear notion of the story's ending, and after gallivanting over the South Seas had to deliver the final chapters. Furthermore, R.L.S. was putting the last touches on a comic novelette, *The Wrong Box,* that he and Lloyd had concocted. He also wrote two ballads of Polynesia, "The Song of Rahero" and "The Feast of Famine," drawn from his South Pacific gleanings.

R.L.S. began taking lessons in the Hawaiian language from Joseph Poepoe, and immersed himself in traditional lore. Six folio sheets of notes have survived in the Huntington Library that suggest he planned an essay on "Kapus, Gods, and Ghosts," but his interest in the multitude of Hawaiian expressions probably soon died down.[9]

Advocates of the "primacy of the Pacific" for the Hawaiian Kingdom hoped that they could use Stevenson for their purposes. From Henry Poor, or even Kalākaua himself, Stevenson heard the story of the Samoan adventure, and after only two weeks in Hawaii the author mailed a fiery letter to the London *Times,*[10] averring that the rickety Hawaiian attempt to intervene among three great powers deserved world respect. Moreover, R.L.S. was enticed into writing an account of the affair that was supposed to be published, along with Joe Strong's photographs, to dramatize Kalākaua's imperialism. "A Samoan Scrapbook" is still in manuscript in the Beinecke Collection, Yale University. Stevenson soon discovered that he had been misled, for in his volume

A Footnote to History (1892) he covers the fiasco in a casual, dry tone. The upshot of his exploitation by the "royal crowd" was that he was involved in Samoan politics many months before he settled in those islands and became the fiery champion of independence for the Samoans.

Stevenson much preferred the beach to the noisy city. The suburb of Waikiki, then a marshy region of rice paddies behind a fringe of shallow beach, could be reached from Honolulu in mule-drawn tram cars. The fare to Kapiolani Park, a quarter of a mile from Manuia Lanai, was ten cents, and there one could hire a hack for twenty-five cents an hour.

At Waikiki, the Stevensons soon moved from Manuia into a straggle of low buildings on property known as the Frank Brown place. One, a small house with a large veranda or lanai, served as dining room and general gathering place. Hung about the lanai were trophies collected in the South Seas—war clubs, carvings, stone axes. The bare walls were draped with tapa cloth and mats. The cottage next door was used by Fanny for her writing and by Lloyd for his painting and photography. The third cottage, which Stevenson called a "grim little shanty,"[11] was his bedroom and workroom combined. It was the domain of cockroaches, spiders, scorpions, and even a friendly mouse that appeared when the author lay in bed playing his flageolet. Swarms of mosquitoes necessitated a netting over the bed, as well as much slapping. A tall fence surrounded this shack and offered some privacy to the struggling writer.

To this hideout R.L.S. retreated when the stream of visitors made it impossible for him to work on the open lanai. Although Wednesday afternoons from two to five had been announced as the Stevenson "at home," people arrived at all hours, and if Fanny did not shield him the usually affable author sometimes had to ask intruders to depart.

Supporting a residence as well as a yacht was a great strain on Stevenson's finances. He decided to send the *Casco* back to San Francisco, and return there by steamer on his journey back to England. Following a farewell dinner aboard, the crew of the *Casco* sailed from Honolulu on February 14.[12] Ah Fu, the Chinese cook who had been signed on in the Marquesas, remained at Waikiki to serve meals while dressed in spotless white attire.

The household garb was usually highly informal. R.L.S. commonly went about the place in flapping pajamas. Fanny, even on the yacht, had adopted the Hawaiian muumuu or gay Mother Hubbard. Louis' mother, however, still dressed primly and seldom abandoned the starched caps she always kept on hand. Lloyd's favorite jacket was a striped blazer. The informality of dress accounts for the story that the Stevensons once accepted a dinner invitation with pleasure, provided Fanny could find her other shoe.

A glimpse of R.L.S. was given by a visitor: "When his callers were admitted, they found a slight man, his coat always of velveteen, who weighed but ninety-eight pounds, and had a hollow chest and a thin body. Long dark hair framed his narrow face, with its blue-veined forehead, its fine long nose, its good chin and smiling mouth. But the glory of his face lay in his dark eyes, which a friend of mine describes as 'burning eyes, such as I've never seen in a human being, as if they looked out from a fiery inside that was consuming him.' " [13]

Stevenson's genius at making acquaintances and adapting his tone to the interests of others brought him many friends who remembered him all the years of their lives. In addition to the royal entourage, including Prince David Kawānanakoa, he knew Allan Herbert, an affable hotel man; Judge Lawrence McCully, associate justice of the supreme court; "Father" Frank Damon, prominent Protestant missionary; and the Honorable Paul Neumann, cabinet member, and his young daughter Anita. R.L.S. sometimes dined at the British Club, and twice he and Lloyd were entertained aboard H.M.S. *Cormorant* [14] as guests of a Lieutenant Pears, an admirer who frequently showed up at Waikiki and once took a flashlight photograph of a typical evening of music around the piano.

The most intimate friends of R.L.S. were Archibald S. Cleghorn and his thirteen-year-old daughter, Princess Ka'iulani. Cleghorn, a former Edinburgh merchant and currently Collector General of Customs, had married Princess Miriam Likelike, late sister of King Kalākaua. During the coming reign of her aunt, Lili'uokalani, Ka'iulani was to be declared heiress-apparent to the throne, but the Revolution of 1893 was to change all that. Ka'iulani was destined to die of pneumonia at 'Āinahau, her Waikiki home, in March 1899, in a Hawaii newly under the American flag.

In 1889, however, the girl was the delight of 'Āinahau, an estate close enough to enable Stevenson to stroll over for a visit. 'Āinahau means "place of the hau tree," but it was widely famed as the site of a spreading banyan. Beneath its shade and drooping aerial roots, R.L.S. would tell the child stories of Scotland, the South Pacific, and lands of fantasy such as only he had visited. As the celebrated peacocks screamed in the green gloom, Ka'iulani spoke of her worry because her father was sending her to Scotland to get the proper schooling for a future queen.

Princess Ka'iulani graciously acted as mistress of her father's household. She visited the Stevensons, and invited them to dinner to enjoy some "good Scotch kaukau [food]." R.L.S. lent her books. April passed all too quickly. After several rounds of formal calls, Cleghorn and his romantic daughter departed on the Oceanic Line steamship *Umatilla* on May 10 for San Francisco. In her autograph album was Stevenson's poem, "Forth from her land to mine she goes," written to cheer her on her way—the best known of the sheaf of verses that R.L.S. wrote in Hawaii. Of all his island friendships, the platonic affair with the half-Scottish princess has most persisted in the imaginations of lovers of Hawaiiana.[15]

Also aboard the *Umatilla* was Mrs. Thomas Stevenson, returning to Scotland to stay with an ailing sister. Her son had changed his plans and decided to risk another cruise to the South Seas. At first it seemed that the only chance for his party to make such a voyage would be to join the missionary vessel *Morning Star IV,* a barkentine with auxiliary steam power. This was a rather dreary prospect for the fun-loving family; they would have to attend prayer services and to follow a prescribed route

rather than choose their own delectable islands, in
which to stay as long as they desired. Fortunately,
Stevenson was able to get a four-month charter for
the trading schooner *Equator*. This vessel had become celebrated as the first to bring to the outside
world the news of the disastrous March 1889 hurricane at Samoa which, as described in a dramatic
Stevenson essay,[16] had ended what otherwise could
have been a three-way sea battle in Apia Harbor.

Stevenson read in the Honolulu newspaper on
April 22 an obituary for Father Damien de Veuster,
Catholic missionary on Molokai, with a long account
of his selfless life taken from the writings of Charles
Warren Stoddard. This word of the death of Damien
on April 15 was a shock to R.L.S., who had determined to meet him on a pilgrimage to the leper
settlement on Molokai. There Damien had ended
his ministries at several churches in the islands, himself a victim of the strange disease that had caused
the Hawaiian authorities to isolate all known cases
on a barren peninsula. Although the author could no
longer meet the priest in the flesh, he planned to visit
the spot where his martyrdom had ended. But before
the Pontifical Mass for the repose of Damien's soul
was celebrated on April 29 at the Cathedral of Our
Lady of Peace in Honolulu, Stevenson was making
a lone tour of the Island of Hawaii, to study a typical
village of the Kona Coast.

Robert Louis Stevenson was not overly fond of the
city of Honolulu. He had an opportunity, in chapter
22 of his novel *The Wrecker,* to give a broad portrayal of this city, but arranged that his narrator
quickly leave the scene. On the other hand, the attrac-

tion of a quiet stretch of the historic Kona region of the Big Island was so great that he preferred it even to the attractions of a live volcano. In a paragraph omitted from the American edition of "The Eight Islands," he explained his choice:

It was on a Saturday afternoon that the steamer *Hall* conveyed me to Ho'okena. She was charged with tourists on their way to the volcano; and I found it hard to justify my choice of a week in an unheard-of hamlet, rather than a visit to one of the admitted marvels of the world. I do not know that I can justify it now and to a larger audience. I should prefer, indeed, to have seen both; but I was at the time embarrassed with arrears of work; it was imperative that I should choose; and I chose one week in a Kona village and another in the lazaretto, and renounced the craters of Mauna Loa and Haleakala. For there are some so constituted as to find a man or a society more curious than the highest mountain; some, in whom the lava foreshores of Kona and Kau will move as deep a wonder as the fiery vents that made them what they are.[17]

The steamer *W. G. Hall* departed from Honolulu on the morning of Friday, April 26, carrying twenty first-class passengers, including Stevenson, and seventy-five deck passengers. Soon the barren western shore of Maui was visible, and thereafter the eastern end, where gashed mountains, nearly five thousand feet high, cast their shadows. Due south rose the humping outline of the island of Lanai. The steamer headed toward the mountains of West Maui, and by sunset approached Lahaina. After leaving that port, the *Hall* ran in the lee of Maui until darkness fell, and then struck out for the Big Island. The conditions on the vessel can only be imagined as she bucked the rough water of the Alenuihaha Channel and the passengers were tossed about in misery.

The steamer sighted Kawaihae Bay in early morning. From the sea, through rain clouds, the peaks of three volcanoes—Mauna Kea, Mauna Loa, and Hualalai—could be glimpsed. At Kailua, the summer residence of King Kalākaua, the *Hall* anchored in the lee of Hualalai and unloaded passengers and goods. Then, south of Kealakekua Bay, where Captain James Cook had met his death on the beach at the hands of infuriated Hawaiian warriors, the *Hall*'s engine stopped and R.L.S. and others were loaded into a whaleboat. He had reached his goal, the hamlet of Ho'okena.

Stevenson's travels on the Kona Coast, around Ho'okena and at the City of Refuge (now a national historical park) are colorfully narrated by himself in "The Eight Islands" and in his journal, here published for the first time. For a whole blessed week he, the only haole or foreigner in a Polynesian community, drank "that warm, light *vin du pays* of human affection" and enjoyed the simple dignity of those about him. He gathered, too, rich material, not only for his sketches but for what is perhaps his most popular short story, "The Bottle Imp."

The *Hall* brought R.L.S. back to "vile Honolulu" on May 3, only one bustling week before he was to say farewell to his mother on the pier where the *Umatilla* was ready to sail. Near exhaustion, he then buckled down and finished *The Master of Ballantrae,* the novel begun in the chill Adirondack Mountains of New York in the winter of 1887. All the while, his thoughts were turning to the island of Molokai.

Undoubtedly he had read *The Lepers of Molokai,*
published in 1885, an account by his friend Stoddard
of a second visit to the colony. Now, in 1889, R.L.S.
bitterly regretted that he had not himself made the
pilgrimage to the peninsula. Had he gone only a
month and a half earlier, he could have seen Father
Damien at work.

To make up for this loss, despite the fear of infection that shook even his brave soul, Stevenson obtained written permission from the Board of Health
and embarked on the *Kilauea Hou* late in the afternoon of May 21. Early next morning he was on deck,
watching the approach to Molokai. The flat, triangular patch of the peninsula of Kalawao, only
ten square miles in area, was cut off on the landward
side by an abrupt, tremendous cliff more than two
thousand feet high. Surely no one could ever escape
from the colony by scaling this grim pali!

Stevenson's adventures on the island of Molokai
are starkly told in his chapters on "The Lazaretto"
and on "The Free Island." He carried a camera on
the trip, but unfortunately any photographs taken
have not survived. The reports he heard of the labors
of Damien so inculcated admiration that many
months later, in Sydney, Australia, he hurled forth
the famed, scathing attack on the Reverend C. M.
Hyde, despite the possibility that a libel suit might
bankrupt him and ruin his family.

"There are Molokais everywhere," R.L.S. con-
cluded as he returned to Honolulu after twelve days
on that island.[18] In the city, one of the first things
he did was to order that a fine $300 piano be sent to
the girls at the Bishop Home on Molokai.

INTRODUCTION

Louis found that Fanny had gone ahead during his absence with preparations for the forthcoming South Sea voyage, purchasing supplies needed for a life far from the comforts of Honolulu. On June 21 the two-masted, eighty-ton schooner *Equator,* under youthful Captain Dennis Reid, anchored off Honolulu Harbor. Next day the Stevensons boarded her to survey their home for the coming months.

The day before their departure, King Kalākaua and two of his cabinet ministers visited the *Equator* for final festivities. The champagne once more flowed freely as the monarch conversed with the Scottish wanderer that he was never to see again. On the day the *Equator* weighed anchor, the king rode up to the pier, laden with leis for all the adventurers, and for Louis an exquisite little model of a schooner with silken sails bearing the inscription: "May the Winds and Waves be Favorable." As the Royal Hawaiian Band played "Aloha 'Oe," the *Equator* made sail for the South Pacific, bearing aboard not only Louis and Fanny but Lloyd Osbourne, Joe Strong, and Ah Fu.

Leaving behind a Hawaii that would never again be the same as described in their letters, the Stevensons headed for the Gilbert group, where they would be the guests of the singular "King Tembinok of Apemama," a monarch that Louis was to immortalize in a sketch. Fortunately, the *Equator* party did not include two sinister brothers, apparently of French nationality, who had vainly begged R.L.S. to take them aboard so that they could go to the South Pacific. Had the gentle author agreed, it is quite likely that these pirates, more evil than any portrayed in *Treasure Island,* would have murdered all his people and thrown them to the sharks, in order to steal the schooner and fulfill their buccaneering dreams, as later they were to do with another vessel.[19]

The achievements of Robert Louis Stevenson during his first stay in the Hawaiian Islands were considerable. Despite frequent interruptions and travels, he was able to finish several volumes and to garner material for later writings, both alone and in collaboration with his stepson and protégé, Lloyd Osbourne.

Beside the Waikiki surf, Stevenson finished rewriting *The Wrong Box* and turned out, not without pain, the final chapters of *The Master of Ballantrae.* He wrote the two ballads using Polynesian legends, "The Song of Rahero" and "The Feast of Famine." On the Kona Coast and Molokai he collected the notes for his chapters on "The Eight Islands," as well as the ammunition to be used in his flaying "Damien letter." He also probably helped his wife write her story, "The Half-White," [20] with a melodramatic plot concerning leprosy that anticipated later writers such as Jack London and James A. Michener.

"The Bottle Imp," according to tradition, was written at Kona—perhaps on Wednesday, May 1. The plot is old in folklore, relating to the devil's granting of perilous wishes, but the adaptation to a Pacific setting is expert, and the number of regional allusions is extensive. "The big house" has the same location as in reality. The name of Keawe, the hero, is derived from the high chief associated with the

City of Refuge, and Keawe's rambles in Honolulu and on the Big Island were limited to those Stevenson had taken by the end of April. The name of Keawe's companion, Lopaka, is a Hawaiian version of "Robert," the first name of Mr. Amalu, the school teacher with whom Stevenson lodged. The ships mentioned were those on which R.L.S. had voyaged. "The Bottle Imp" was considered by its author to be "one of my best works, and ill to equal." [21] His judgment has been confirmed by most critics.

"The Isle of Voices," another story of magic, deriving from an Oriental myth, has as its main character a Hawaiian named Keola, married to the daughter of Kalamake, a sorcerer of the island of Molokai who was able to obtain shining dollars on the beach of an island farther to the south. Along with "The Bottle Imp" and "The Beach of Falesá," it comprised the volume called *Island Nights' Entertainments* (1893), three short stories redolent of the South Seas in the nineteenth century.

The arrival in Honolulu on April 6 of the fishing schooner *Norma* gave the newspapers a fascinating mystery story. The vessel had picked up Captain F. D. Walker, his family, and the crew of the *Wandering Minstrel,* survivors for fourteen months of a wreck on Midway Island, a thousand miles to the northwest. This incident was the germ of the novel *The Wrecker* (1892), by R.L.S. and Lloyd Osbourne. The main character, Loudon Dodd, strongly resembles Stevenson himself. The plot of this book differs somewhat from the saga of the *Minstrel,* a lengthy and complicated episode never sufficiently explained. The rumor that the captain of the *Norma* had demanded all of Walker's money in return for rescuing the party gave the collaborators the solution to their problem of motivating the seizure of a ship by a desperate band of castaways. Although much of the action of *The Wrecker* takes place elsewhere than among the Pacific islands, it is one of the best fictional accounts of voyaging in this ocean.[22]

Another collaboration by the author and his stepson was in progress on the cruise south from Hawaii. This was originally titled *The Pearl Fisher,* but was published in 1894 as *The Ebb-Tide: A Trio and a Quartette.* This novelette dealing with three beachcombers who steal a schooner and escape from Tahiti only to be outsmarted by a zealot on a secret island contains, among other South Sea portraits, the depiction of the cockney Huish, a scoundrel who would make Long John Silver look like a nursery bogey.

Stevenson envisioned a grand design for his Pacific writing. Before the *Equator* arrived at Samoa, he wrote to Sidney Colvin outlining his magnum opus, a big book he planned to call *The South Seas,* which would run to sixty chapters. "If I can execute what is designed," he declared, "there are few better books now extant on this globe, bar the epics, and the big tragedies, and histories, and the choice lyric poetics and a novel or so—none. . . . At least nobody has had such stuff; such wild stories, such beautiful scenes, such singular intimacies, such manners and traditions, so incredible a mixture of the beautiful and horrible, the savage and civilized." [23]

The main theme of this "prose-epic," as Stevenson stated it in an interview several years later, would be "the unjust (yet I can see the inevitable) extinction of the Polynesian Islanders by our shabby civilization. In such a plan I will, of course, make liberal use of the civilized element, but in the most and best the story shall remain distinctively Polynesian." [24]

Part I of the big book, fetchingly titled "Of Schooners, Islands, and Maroons," was never completed. Neither was Part IV on Tahiti. Parts II, III, and VI, on the Marquesas, the Tuamotus, and the Gilberts, finally emerged as *In the South Seas* (1896). Part VII, on Samoa—a group he had not yet visited—eventually became *A Footnote to History*. Part V, "The Eight Islands," was to include a chapter on "Missions," never published; a five-part chapter on the Kona Coast of Hawaii; and a four-part chapter on Molokai. These five chapters of the contemplated work appeared as a series of letters to the New York *Sun* in 1891 but were omitted from almost all editions of Stevenson's collected works. They are here retrieved from near oblivion for the enjoyment of readers who have visited America's fiftieth state or wish to do so, as well as for followers of the career and writings of a beloved British author.

Stevenson's wife had already become alarmed about the possibility that Louis had forsaken his true genius—the portrayal of living and breathing human beings—and would become bogged down in linguistics and archaeology. As she had written to Sidney Colvin previously: "Louis has the most enchanting material that anyone ever had in the whole world for his book, and I am afraid he is going to spoil it all. He has taken into his Scotch Stevenson head that a stern duty lies before him, and that his book must be a sort of scientific and historical impersonal thing . . . leaving out all he knows of the people themselves. And I believe there is no one living who has got so near to them, or who understands them as he does. . . . What a thing it is to have a 'man of genius' to deal with." [25] Neither Fanny nor Colvin, however, could deflect R.L.S. from his effort to write the great Pacific epic.

During later Pacific travels and sojourns, Stevenson did not forget his Arcadian months in Hawaii. He ordered that a set of his works be sent to King Kalākaua. When he heard of the death of the king and of the accession of Liliʻuokalani, he wrote from Apia, Samoa, in March 1891, offering his sympathy and some advice, auguring well for a Hawaii "where much is sure to be effected by a firm, kind, serious, and not harsh sovereign." [26]

The Stevensons cruised on the *Equator* through the Gilberts and at last came to Apia on the Samoan island of Upolu, where for the first time R.L.S. was greeted with the sobriquet of "Tusitala" and where he bought three hundred acres of forest land under Mount Vaea, on which his final home would be built.

It was in Sydney, Australia, in February 1890, that R.L.S. read in a religious paper a copy of the letter that Dr. C. M. Hyde had written concerning Father Damien, and fired off his searing reply. He could not have anticipated that the letter would be eagerly seized upon by the royalist faction in Honolulu, who represented it as the opening gun of a campaign by a staunch loyalist and used it as ammunition against the increasing political power of the Protestant, missionary-born Reform Party.

Again illness struck Stevenson, and again a sea voyage was prescribed. The *Janet Nicoll* took the couple, along with Lloyd, to Auckland and Apia, and then eastward to the islands of Penrhyn, Manihiki, Suwarrow, and Nassau. They cruised the Tokelau and Ellice groups, and once more the Gilberts, and then sailed to the big Melanesian island of New Caledonia. Back in Sydney, the party separated. Lloyd left for England, and the Stevensons headed in October for Apia, to live in the little cottage on their half-cleared upland estate while the great house of Vailima was being built.

R.L.S. returned to Hawaii in the autumn of 1893, to accompany his cousin and biographer, Graham Balfour, as far as Honolulu on a homeward voyage. Louis went for a short pleasure trip and did not intend to stay long, but his fate ruled otherwise.

The Hawaiian scene had changed greatly in less than four years. The Merry Monarch no longer reigned over parties in his boathouse. His sister Lili'uokalani, who had succeeded Kalākaua, had been deposed in a bloodless revolution led by pro-American annexationists. Annexation had been delayed, however, by a change of administration in the White House, and a provisional government led by Sanford Ballard Dole was in the process of becoming the Republic of Hawaii. Lili'uokalani was living quietly in Washington Place, and Princess Ka'iulani was far away in England. Stevenson was never at a loss for friends, however, and made new ones even though the gay *Casco* days were over and he planned soon to return to Samoa.

Stevenson and Balfour arrived at Honolulu aboard the S.S. *Mariposa* on September 20. R.L.S. planned to see off his cousin in a week and return to Samoa at once on the *Alameda*. He had brought with him his Samoan house boy, Taalolo, who had contracted the measles on the ship. This disease, often fatal to Polynesians, required strict quarantine. By special permission, the boy was allowed to land with Stevenson and drive with him to Waikiki, where he was put under guard in Windmill Cottage on the grounds of the Sans Souci Hotel.

This rambling hostelry on the beach, beneath towering coconut palms, was managed in 1893 by George Lycurgus. Born in Greece before the American Civil War, Lycurgus was destined to live more than a century and to preside in his later years over his beloved Volcano House, the famed hotel overlooking the crater of Kilauea on the Big Island. Tall and craggy, Lycurgus had first visited Honolulu in 1889 and had recently settled at Waikiki. Of Stevenson, Lycurgus recalled: "He wrote mostly at night, filling dozens of pages with writing and scattering paper over the floor. He was always the gentleman, always ready with a story but yet apparently eager to listen to the tales of others." [27]

The main building comprised a large lanai used as lounge, dining room, and kitchen. Many of the panel decorations had been painted by Belle and Joe Strong. The residents were given small thatched bungalows about ten by twelve feet, most of the space taken up by a bed. R.L.S. chose Bella Vista Cottage,

INTRODUCTION

and prepared to enjoy life in Honolulu free from the pressure of fulfilling literary assignments.

He called on ex-Queen Lili'uokalani but kept away from the officials of the provisional government who were installed in Iolani Palace. He picked up his former friendships with Allan Herbert and A. S. Cleghorn, and made new acquaintances at the Royal Hawaiian Hotel and the Pacific Club.

Soon after his arrival, a committee invited him to address the Honolulu Scottish Thistle Club. He was delighted to accept, and on the evening of September 27 appeared in the clubrooms on Merchant Street, dressed in a dashing suit of brown corduroy brightened with his favorite red sash. His spirited recapitulation of centuries of Scottish history before a capacity crowd made his listeners forget the eccentricities of the emaciated lecturer, who had only a year longer to live. He ended with the mention that he had been affected by the recent dedication to him of *The Stickit Minister,* a book by the Scottish author S. N. Crockett, with a poignant mention of those places

> Where about the graves of the martyrs the
> whaups are crying,
> My heart remembers how!

He added: "I feel that when I shall come to die out here among these beautiful islands, I shall have lost something that had been my due—my native, predestinate, and forfeited grave among honest Scots sods."

Next day, planning to leave on the *Alameda* after having seen off his cousin on the *Oceanic* the day before, Stevenson rose early and awaited the hackman Quinn, who had also been his driver in 1889. Quinn had bought a new horse to celebrate the occasion of departure. No sooner was the author seated than the raw creature bolted. The two men faced instant death as the horse raced down a narrow, winding road for a mile and a half. R.L.S. sat erect and grim on the back seat, white as a ghost. Not until they had come two miles nearer town did Stevenson begin to address his driver at length: "O Quinn, brave and witty jehu, I don't like this new animal of yours; I have an idea he is a bit of a politician, like yourself, and is apt to take the bit in his teeth. . . ." [28]

R.L.S. was so shaken that he canceled his departure and returned to Sans Souci, where he was confined to his bed for a fortnight. The unlucky jehu Quinn also went to bed—with the measles, caught from Taalolo on the day when he had driven the pair to Waikiki. Fortunately, the Samoan lad by now had recovered and was able to attend the ill author, who was under the care of Dr. George Trousseau, formerly Kalākaua's royal physician. Stevenson sent word of his disability to his wife, knowing that she would take the first steamer from Samoa to rescue him. She arrived from Apia on October 19 on the R.M.S.S. *Monowai,* and at once took charge.

By then Louis had recovered sufficiently to promise to address an informal meeting of the Thistle Club on October 21, but his careful wife, abetted by Dr. Trousseau, canceled all engagements. Her husband sent an amusing note to the newspaper. [29] He and Fanny had moved into two rooms at the eastern end of Luce Cottage, and it was there that Allen Hutchinson, an English sculptor in the islands, took a cast for the bronze bust of Stevenson that is now a proud possession of the Honolulu Academy of Arts. It is the only bust of Stevenson made during his lifetime.

When Taalolo had recovered from the measles, R.L.S., who had a strong affection for him, sent him on a sightseeing trip. He also sent him with messages to Lili'uokalani and others, to help him find his way about. Before leaving, R.L.S. purchased a fine ring for Taalolo to wear back to Samoa.

The editor of the *Pacific Commercial Advertiser*, Arthur Johnstone, had printed a note highly praising the Thistle Club lecture. When Stevenson recovered, he visited Johnstone's office to thank him, and the two discussed the difficulties of writing about Pacific islanders. At the editor's request, R.L.S. wrote for publication in the paper a poem called "The High Winds of Nuuanu," concerning the steady blast on the Nuuanu Pali that has disheveled thousands of visitors to that blowy spot above Honolulu.[30]

About a week after he became ill, R.L.S. had written a letter to be published in the *Advertiser*. For some reason, the Sans Souci Hotel had been given the label around town of a "disorderly house." Always ready to spring to the defense, Stevenson attempted to silence critics by his letter of October 6, which assured prospective guests that there was "no quieter haven"—except for a disturbing midnight ringing of the telephone in the dining room, a modern invasion of his privacy that he was never able to accept.[31] Apparently, during his period of fever, Stevenson had been moved to "the heart of the establishment, opening upon all the public rooms."

The last piece of writing done by Stevenson in Hawaii was an entry in the Sans Souci register as he stood in his cape ready to depart. It appeared as an advertisement[32] in the newspapers the following week:

If anyone desire such old-fashioned things as lovely scenery, quiet, pure air, clear sea water, good food, and heavenly sunsets hung out before his eyes over the Pacific and the distant hills of Waianae, I recommend him cordially to the "Sans Souci."

ROBERT LOUIS STEVENSON
T. A. SIMPSON, MANAGER

The Thistle Club, at its meeting of October 23, had elected Stevenson "honorary chieftain." A little silver emblem was pinned on his lapel the day before his departure. He promised that it would be buried with him, and it was.

Quietly, on the S.S. *Mariposa* on the afternoon of Friday, October 27, Stevenson left Honolulu for the last time. The king was dead and the Royal Hawaiian Band did not play on the wharf, but R.L.S. left behind many friends who would long remember his visit. Archibald Cleghorn remained in Stevenson's stateroom for a last chat. As his friend rose to go, R.L.S. warmly shook hands and said, "Now, Cleghorn, if I can be of any service to the royal cause in Hawaii, just drop me a line, and I will come right back here." [33]

But it was too late for publicists to win over politicians. Hawaii was fated to become part of an expanding United States, and Stevenson was fated to live only a little more than one year longer, even in the equable climate of the Pacific islands. Had he returned to cold Europe or the eastern states, he perhaps would have perished years earlier. As it was, he died in December 1894, not of his lung ailment but of a sudden brain hemorrhage in his comfortable big house above Apia. Husky Samoan chiefs bore his coffin to the top of Mount Vaea where he lies today under a concrete monument inscribed with the final lines of the epitaph he had written, despairing, in San Francisco thirteen years earlier:

> Home is the sailor, home from the sea,
> And the hunter home from the hill.

The sailor and hunter had reached dramatic fulfillment in the Pacific region. His six-month stay in Hawaii in 1889 and his five-week visit in 1893 had given him not only literary material but friendships and a renewed zest for living, as well as a compassion that reached its peak on the somber island of Molokai. A master of the author's craft, he felt that, even with a lifetime burden of illness, he should have been able to achieve more than one career. In his last year he wrote to his longtime friend Will H. Low: "I could have wished to be otherwise busy in this world. I ought to have been able to build lighthouses and write *David Balfour* too." [34]

Robert Louis Stevenson, that brave, gentle man, will not soon be forgotten in the Hawaii he loved.

NOTES ON INTRODUCTION

1. *See* Letter No. 3.

2. *Works,* Vailima edition (London: Heinemann, 1922–23), 9:25. (This is not the Vailima edition of Note 5.)

3. Ibid., p. 8.

4. *Hawaiian Life* (Chicago and New York: F. Tennyson Neely, 1894), p. 115. Stevenson characterized King Kalākaua, in *A Footnote to History* (*Works,* Swanston edition [London: Chatto & Windus, 1912], 17:36) as "that amiable, far from unaccomplished, but too convivial sovereign."

5. *The South Seas, Works,* Vailima edition (New York: P. F. Collier & Son Co., 1912), 9:23.

6. *See* Letter No. 2.

7. W. D. Alexander, *History of the Later Years of the Monarchy and the Hawaiian Revolution of 1893* (Honolulu: Hawaiian Gazette Co., 1896), p. 16.

8. Sidney Colvin, ed., *The Letters of Robert Louis Stevenson* (New York: Charles Scribner's Sons, 1911), 4:227 (hereinafter given as *Letters*).

9. Huntington Library Manuscript HM 20534. Two pages of terms in Hawaiian and English are headed "General"; another page is headed "Divisions of land and sea"; and three pages are headed "Hawaii: Kapus, Gods and Ghosts." Probably the Hawaiian terms were given by Joseph Poepoe and the English definitions derived from Lorrin Andrews, *A Dictionary of the Hawaiian Language* (Honolulu: Henry M. Whitney, 1865).

10. It appeared on February 10, 1890.

11. Letter No. 6 gives a full description and plan of the estate.

12. Next day the following note appeared in the *Pacific Commercial Advertiser:* "Mr. and Mrs. Robert Louis Stevenson did

not leave in the yacht, 'Casco,' that brought them here from the South Seas and sailed yesterday for San Francisco. It will afford the community pleasure to learn that the distinguished author will prolong his stay perhaps three months in this Paradise of the Pacific."

13. From a lecture by Mrs. Mabel Wing Castle in Arthur Johnstone, *Recollections of Robert Louis Stevenson in the Pacific* (London: Chatto & Windus, 1905), pp. 56–57 (hereinafter given as Johnstone).

14. The *Cormorant* was probably the pattern for the vessel called H.M.S. *Tempest* in Stevenson's novel *The Wrecker*.

15. The Cleghorn estate, situated across Kalakaua Avenue from Waikiki Beach and inland from the present Princess Kaiulani Hotel, has vanished under modern construction in Waikiki. At Cleghorn's death in 1910, his will left the grounds, to be used as a park, to the Territory of Hawaii with certain restrictions. The legislature did not accept the offer. The land was bought in 1917 and subdivided. The history of the banyan tree, planted by Cleghorn himself, is given in Sister Martha Mary McGaw, *Stevenson in Hawaii* (Honolulu: University of Hawaii Press, 1950), pp. 146–147 (hereinafter given as McGaw). The tree was cut down in 1949; the bronze plaque is now treasured by the Kaiulani School on North King Street in Honolulu. Cleghorn Street and Kaiulani Street are found in Waikiki, near Tusitala Street—named for the Samoan sobriquet of R.L.S., "teller of tales." The grass shack called the Stevenson Hut on the grounds of Waioli Tea Room in Manoa Valley was purchased by a resident from the 'Āinahau Estate and given to the Salvation Army; it is a popular shrine, although Stevenson may never have stepped inside it.

16. *A Footnote to History* (London: Cassell, 1892), Chapter 10.

17. Swanston edition (London: Chatto & Windus, 1912), 18:189.

18. *See* Letter No. 19.

19. *See* A. Grove Day, *Adventurers of the Pacific* (New York: Meredith Press, 1969), Chapter 8, "The Brothers Rorique: Pirates De Luxe."

20. *Scribner's Magazine,* 9:282–288 (March 1891).

21. To Sidney Colvin, *Letters,* 4:168.

22. Accounts appeared in the *Pacific Commercial Advertiser* for April 8 and June 13, 1889. The latter item must have aroused R.L.S. to action. *See* Letter No. 19: "I am going down now to

get the story of a shipwrecked family, who were fifteen months on an island with a murderer." "The captain of the rescuing vessel first ascertained exactly what amount of money had been saved from the wreck," recalled Mrs. Stevenson; "it was just this sum, several thousand dollars—comprising all the sailors' wages as well as the entire means of the captain—that the stranger demanded as his price for carrying the miserable creatures to the nearest civilized port, where they were dumped, penniless, on the wharf. . . . My husband and my son had been continually recurring, in their talk, to the mystery of the *Wandering Minstrel*; it now struck them that they might collaborate on a novel, founded on the episode of the wreck. One fine moonlight night, the fresh trade wind blowing in their faces, the two men sat late on deck, inventing the plot of *The Wrecker*." Prefatory note, Vailima edition (New York: Charles Scribner's Sons, 1922), 17:7, 10.

23. To Sidney Colvin, *Letters*, 3:164.

24. Johnstone, p. 103.

25. *See* Letter No. 16.

26. The letter appeared in the Honolulu *Advertiser* for January 11, 1925.

27. Tom O'Brien, "The Old Man of the Mountain," Honolulu *Advertiser*, Sunday Polynesian, August 17, 1947, p. 2.

28. Johnstone, p. 123.

29. *See* Letter No. 24.

30. Stevenson did not finish the poem in time to present it in the paper, and it first appeared in Johnstone, pp. 307–308.

31. *See* Letter No. 23.

32. McGaw, p. 134.

33. Johnstone, pp. 141–142.

34. *Letters*, 4:284.

I

THE EIGHT ISLANDS

THE EIGHT ISLANDS

The travel sketches that appear in certain editions of Stevenson's volume In the South Seas *under the title of "The Eight Islands" deal mainly with his tour of the Kona Coast and the City of Refuge (now a national historical park) and with his visit to the isolation station for lepers on the peninsula of Kalawao, part of the island of Molokai. These regions are much better known to visitors today than they were in 1889, and the footsteps of R.L.S. can more easily be retraced.*

Originally, Stevenson's letters from the South Seas appeared in the New York Sun *from February 6 to December 13, 1891, and almost simultaneously in* Black and White *in England. Most of these letters were later printed in book form with the title* In the South Seas, *but the sketches about the Hawaiian Kingdom were usually not included because Stevenson had expressed some dissatisfaction with them.*

The Swanston Edition of the complete works, printed in 1911 (London: Chatto & Windus, 25 vol.), contains in Vol. 18, In the South Seas, *the sketches concerning the tour of the Kona Coast, arranged in five chapters. In the Vailima Edition*

3

TRAVELS IN HAWAII

(*New York: P. F. Collier & Son Co., 1912, 9 vol.*),
the letters appear in Vol. 9, The South Seas, *pages
152–204, "complete and entire as first written." This
is the text that has been followed in the nine chapters
below. The paragraphing of the Hawaiian essays
differs from that of the Swanston Edition, and the
five sketches on the tour of Kona appear as three; all
are dated "Upolu, Samoan Islands, December,
1890." The paragraph in which R.L.S. gives his
reason for making the trip to Kona is omitted, and
occasional phrases have been added or deleted. The
four essays about Molokai appear in this volume for
the first time; they are all dated at Upolu in January
1891. These chapters also appear in a quite different
Vailima Edition, limited to 1030 numbered copies
(New York: Charles Scribner's Sons, 1922, 26
vol.), in Vol. 26,* Miscellaneous, *pages 454–476.
This edition is especially useful because it contains
photographs and occasional prefatory notes by Mrs.
Stevenson.*

*A Hawaiian leper escaped from Molokai and,
somehow finding his way over the ocean for hundreds of miles to the south, started a plague on the
island of Penrhyn or Tongareva in the Tokelau
group. This story, taken from pages 432–435 of the
same volume, here forms chapter 10 of the sketches
and shows an aftermath of Stevenson's visit to
Molokai.*

✝ 1 ✝

THE KONA COAST

Of the island of Hawaii, though I have passed days becalmed under its lee, and spent a week upon its shores, I have never yet beheld the profile. Dense clouds continued to enshroud it far below its middle; not only the zone of snow and fire, but a great part of the forest region was covered or at least veiled by a perpetual rain. And yet even on my first sight, beholding so little and that through a glass from the deck of the *Casco,* the rude Plutonic structure of the isle was conspicuous. Here was none of the accustomed glitter of the beach, none of the close shoreside forests of the typical high island. All seemed black and barren, and to slope sheer into the sea. Unexpected movements of the land caught the attention: folds that glittered with a certain vitreosity; black mouths of caves; ranges of low cliffs, vigorously designed a while in sun and shadow, and that sank again into the general declivity of the island glacis. Under its gigantic cowl of cloud the coast frowned upon us with a face of desolation.

On my return I passed from a humming city, with shops and palaces and busy wharfs, plying cabs and tramcars, telephones in operation and a railway in building; mounted a strong and comfortable local steamer; sailed under desolate shores indeed, but guided in the night by sea and harbor lights, and was set down at last in a village uninhabited by any white, the creature of pure native taste—of which, what am I to say but that I know no such village in Europe? A well-to-do Western hamlet in the States would be the closest parallel; and it is a moderate prophecy to call it so already.

Ho'okena is its name. It stands on the same coast which I had wondered at before from the tossing *Casco,* the same coast on which the far-voyager Cook ended a noble career not very nobly. That district of Kona where he fell is one illustrious in the history of Hawaii. It was at first the center of the dominion of the great Kamehameha.

There, in an unknown sepulcher, his bones are still hidden; there, too, his reputed treasures, spoils of a buccaneer, lie and are still vainly sought for, in one of the thousand caverns of the lava. There the tabus were first broken, there the missionaries first received; and, but for the new use of ships and the new need of harbors, here might be still the chief city and the organs of the kingdom. Yet a nearer approach confirmed the impression of the distance. It presents to the seaward one immense decline. Streams of lava have followed and submerged each other down this slope, and overflowed into the sea. These cooled and shrank, and were buried under fresh inundations, or dislocated by fresh tremors of the mountain. A multiplicity of caves is the result. The mouths of caves are everywhere; the lava is tunneled with corridors and halls; under houses high on the mountain the sea can be heard throbbing in the bowels of the land, and there is one gallery of miles which has been used by armies as a pass. Streams are thus unknown. The rain falls continually in the highlands; an isle that rises nearly fourteen thousand feet sheer from the sea could never fail of rain, but the treasure is squandered on a sieve, and by sunless conduits returns unseen into the ocean. Corrugated slopes of lava, bristling lava cliffs, sprouts of metallic clinkers, miles of coast without a well or rivulet, scarce anywhere a beach, nowhere a harbor—here seems a singular land to be contended for in battle as a seat for courts and princes. Yet it possessed in the eyes of the natives one more than countervailing advantage. The windward shores of the isle are beaten by a monstrous surf; there are places where goods and passengers must be hauled up and lowered by a rope; there are coves which even the daring boatmen of Hamakua dread to enter; and men live isolated in their hamlets or communicate by giddy footpaths in the cliff. Upon the side of Kona the tablelike margin of the lava affords almost everywhere a passage by land, and the waves, reduced by the vast breakwater of the island, allow an almost continual communication by way of sea. Yet even here the surf of the Pacific appears formidable to the stranger as he lands, and daily delights him with its beauty as he walks the shore.

The land and sea breezes alternate on the Kona Coast with regularity, and the veil of rain draws up and down the talus of the mountain—now retiring to the zone of forests, now descending to the margin of the sea. It was in one of the latter and rarer moments that I was set on board a whaleboat full of intermingled barrels, passengers, and oarsmen. The rain fell and blotted the crude and somber colors of the scene. The coast rose but a little way; it was then intercepted by the cloud; and, for all that appeared, we might have been landing on an isle of some two hundred feet of elevation. On the immediate foreshore, under a low cliff, there stood some score of houses, trellised and verandaed, set in narrow gardens, and painted gaudily in green and white; the whole surrounded and shaded by a grove of coco palms and fruit trees, springing (as by miracle) from the bare lava. In front, the population of the neighborhood were gathered for the weekly incident, the passage of the steamer, sixty to eighty strong, and attended by a disproportionate allowance of horses, mules, and donkeys; for this land of rock is, singular to say, a land of breeding. The green trees, the painted houses, the gay dresses of the women, were everywhere relieved on the uncompromising blackness of the lava; and the rain which fell, unheeded by the sightseers, blended and beautified the contrast.

The boat was run in upon a breaker and we passengers ejected on a flat rock, where the next wave submerged us to the knees. There we continued to stand, the rain drenching us from above, the sea from below, like people mesmerized; and as we were all (being travelers) tricked out with the green garlands of departure, we must have offered somewhat the same appearance as a shipwrecked picnic. The purser spied and introduced me to my host, ex-Judge Nahinu, who was then deep in business, despatching and receiving goods. He was dressed in pearl-gray tweed, like any self-respecting Englishman, only the band of his wide-awake was made of peacock's feather.

"House by and by," said he, his English being limited, and carried me to the shelter of a rather lofty shed. On three sides it was open, on the fourth closed by a house. It was reached from without by five or six wooden steps. On the fourth side a further flight of ten conducted to the balcony of the house. A table spread with goods divided it across, so that I knew it for the village store and (according to the laws that rule in country life) the village lounging place. People sat with dangling feet along the house veranda; they sat on benches on the level of the shed or among the goods upon the counter; they came and went, they talked and waited; they opened, skimmed, and pocketed half-read their letters; they opened the journal, and found a moment, not for the news, but for the current number of the story—methought, I might have been in France, and the paper the *Petit Journal* instead of the *Nupepa Eleele*. On other islands I had been the center of attention; here none observed my presence. One hundred and ten years before the ancestors of these indifferents had looked in the faces of Cook and his seamen with admiration and alarm; called them gods, called them volcanoes; took their clothes for a loose skin, confounded their hats and their heads, and described their pockets as a "treasure door, through which they plunge their hands into their bodies and bring forth cutlery and necklaces and cloth and nails"; and today the coming of the most attractive stranger failed (it would appear) to divert them from Miss Porter's *Scottish Chiefs,* for that was the novel of the day—*Na 'Lii O Sekotia*—so ran the title in Hawaii.

My host returned, and led me round the shore among the mules and donkeys to his house. Like all the houses of the hamlet, it was on the European, or to be more descriptive, on the American plan. The parlor was fitted with the usual furniture, and ornamented with the portraits of Kamehameha the Third, Lunalilo, Kalākaua, the queen consort of the isles, and Queen Victoria. There was a Bible on the table; other books stood on a shelf. A comfortable bedroom was placed at my service, the welcome afforded me was cordial and unembarrassed, the food good and plentiful. My host, my hostess, his grown daughters, strapping lassies, his young hopefuls, misbehaving at a meal or perfunctorily employed upon their schoolbooks; all that I found in that house, beyond the speech and a few exotic dishes on the table, would have been familiar and exemplary in Europe.

I walked that night beside the sea. The steamer, with its lights and crowd of tourists, was gone by; it had left me alone among these aliens, and I felt no touch of strangeness. The trim, lamplit houses shining quietly, like villas, each in its narrow garden; the gentle sound of speech from within; the room that awaited my return, with the lamp and the books and the spectacled householder studying his Bible—there was nothing changed; it was in such conditions I had myself grown up and played, a child, beside the borders of another sea. And some ten miles from where I walked Cook was adored as a deity; his bones, when he was dead, were cleansed for worship; his entrails devoured in a mistake by rambling children.

A day of session in the Ho'okena Court House equally surprised me. The judge, a very intelligent, serious Hawaiian, sat behind a table, taking careful notes, two policemen, with their bright metal badges, standing attention at his back or bustling forth on errands. The plaintiff was a Portuguese. For years he had kept store and raised cattle in the district without trouble or dispute. His store stood always open—it was standing so, seven miles away, at the moment of the case—and when his cattle strayed they were duly impounded and restored to him on payment of one shilling. But recently a gentleman of great acuteness and a thousand imperfect talents had married into the family of a neighboring proprietor, consecutively on which event the storekeeper's cattle began to be detained and starved, the fine rose to half a dollar, and lastly a cow had disappeared. The Portuguese may have been right or wrong; he was convinced the newcomer was the mainspring of the change; called a suit in consequence against the father-in-law, and it was the son-in-law who appeared for the defense. I saw him there seated at his ease, with spectacles on brow, still young, much of a gentleman in looks, and dressed in faultless European clothes; and presently, for my good fortune, he arose to address the court. It appears he has already stood for the Hawaiian Parliament, but the people (I was told) "did not think him honest," and he was defeated. Honesty, to our ways of thought, appears a trifle in a candidate, and I think we have few con-

stituents to refuse so great a charmer. I understood
but a few dozen words, yet I heard the man with
delight, followed the junctures of his argument, knew
when he was enumerating points in his own favor,
when he was admitting those against him, when he
was putting a question *per absurdum,* when (after the
due pause) he smilingly replied to it. There was no
haste, no heat, no prejudice; with a hinted gesture,
with a semitone of intonation, the speaker lightly set
forth and underlined the processes of reason; he could
not shift a foot or touch his spectacles but what persuasion radiated in the court; it is impossible to conceive a style of oratory more rational or civilized. The
point to which he spoke was pretty in itself. The
people, as I had been told, did not think the orator
honest; some judge, on a particular occasion, had inclined to the same view, and the man of talent was
disbarred. By a clause in a statute, a layman or a disbarred lawyer might conduct a case for himself or
for one of "his own family." Is a father-in-law one
of a man's own family? "Yes," argued the orator.
"No," with less grace and perspicuity, Nahinu, retained by the Portuguese. The laws of the tight little
kingdom are conceived in duplicate for the Hawaiian
hare and his many white friends. The native text
appearing inconclusive, an appeal was made to the
English, and I (as *amicus curiae*) led out, installed
upon the court house steps, and painfully examined
as to its precise significance. The judge heard the
orator; he heard Nahinu; he received by the mouth
of the schoolmaster my report, for which he thanked
me with a bow, and ruled the claimant out. This
skirmish decided the fate of the engagement; fortune

was faithful to the Portuguese, and late in the afternoon the capable judge rode off homeward with his portfolio under his arm. No court could have been more equally and decently conducted; judge, parties, lawyers, and police were all decorous and competent, and but for the plaintiff, the business was entirely native.

The Portuguese had come seven miles to Ho'okena, sure of substantial justice, and he left his store open, fearless of being robbed. Another white man of strong sense and much frugality and choler thus reckoned up what he had lost by theft in thirty-nine years among the different islands of Hawaii. A pair of shoes, an umbrella, some feet of hose pipe, and one batch of chickens. It is his continual practice to send Hawaiians by a perilous, solitary path with sums in specie; at any moment the messenger might slip, the money bag roll down a thousand feet of precipice, and lodge in fissures inaccessible to men; and consider how easy it were to invent such misadventures! "I should have to know a white man well before I trusted him," he said; "I trust Hawaiians without fear. It would be villainous of me to say less." It should be remembered the Hawaiians of yore were not particular; they were eager to steal from Cook, whom they believed to be a god, and it was a theft that led to the tragedy at Kealakekua Bay; and it must not be forgotten that the Hawaiians of today are many of them poor. One residual trait of savage incompetence I have already referred to: they can not administer a trust. I was told there had never yet been a case known. Even a judge, skilled in the knowledge of the law and upright in its administration, was found insusceptible of those duties and distinctions which appear so natural and come so easy to the European. But the disability stands alone, a single survival in the midst of change, and the faults of the modern Hawaiian incline to the other side. My orator of Ho'okena courtroom may be a gentleman much maligned; I may have received his character from the lips of his political opponents, but the type described is common. The islands begin to fill with lawyers, many of whom, justly or unjustly, are disbarred, and to the age of Kamehameha, the age of Glossin [a knavish lawyer in a Walter Scott novel] has succeeded. Thus none would rob the store of the Portuguese, but the law was wrested to oppress him.

It was of old a warlike and industrious race. They were diggers and builders; the isles are still full of their deserted monuments; the modern word of law, *kānāwai,* "water rights," still serves to remind us of their ancient irrigation. And the island story is compact of battles. Their courage and good will to labor seem now confined to the sea, where they are active sailors and fearless boatmen, pursue the shark in his own element, and make a pastime of their incomparable surf. On shore they flee equally from toil and peril, and are all turned to carpet occupations and to parlous frauds. Nahinu, an ex-judge, was paid but two dollars for a hard day in court, and he is paying one dollar a day to the laborers among his coffee. All Hawaiians envy and are ready to compete with him for this odd chance of an occasional fee for some hours' talking; he cannot find one to earn a certain hire under the sun in his plantation, and the work is all transacted by immigrant Chinese. One cannot but be reminded of the love of the French middle class for office work; but in Hawaii it is the race in bulk that shrinks from manly occupation. During a late revolution a lady found a powerful young Hawaiian crouching among the grass in her garden. "What are you doing there?" she cried, for she was a strong partisan. "Do you not know they are murdering your King?" "I know," said the skulker. "Why do you not go to help him?" she asked. "Aflaid," said the poor craven, and crouched again among the grass. Here was a strange grandchild for the warriors that followed or faced Kamehameha. I give the singular instance as the more explicit; but the whole race must have been stricken at the moment with a similar weakness. No man dare say of this revolution that it was unprovoked; but its means were treachery and violence; the numbers and position of those engaged made the design one of the most insolent in history; and a mere modicum of native boldness and cohesion must have brought it to the dust. "My race had one virtue, they were brave," said a typical Hawaiian, "and now they have taken that away."

I have named a French example; but the thought that haunts the stranger in Hawaii is that of Italy. The ruggedness of feature which marks out the race among Polynesians is the Italian ruggedness. Countenances of the same eloquent harshness, manners of the same vivacious cordiality, are to be found in Hawaii and among Italian fisherfolk. I know no race that carries years more handsomely, whose people, in the middle way of life, retain more charm. I recall faces, both of men and women, with a certain leonine stamp, trusty, sagacious, brave, beautiful in plainness; faces that take the heart captive. The tougher struggle of the race in these hard isles has written history there; energy enlivens the Hawaiian strength. Or did so once, and the faces are still eloquent of the lost possession. The stock that has produced a Cæsar, a Kamehameha, a Ka'ahumanu, retains their signature.

※ 2 ※

A RIDE IN THE FOREST

By the Hawaiian tongue, the slope of these steep islands is parceled out in zones. As we mount from the seaboard we pass by the region of Ilima, named for a flowering shrub, and the region of *'Āpaʻa,* named for a wind, to *Maʻū,* the place of mist. This has a secondary name, the *Au-* or *Wao-kanaka,* "the place of men" by exclusion, man not dwelling higher. The next, accordingly, is called the *Wao Akua,* region of gods and goblins; other names, some apparently involving thoughts of solitude and danger, follow till the top is reached. The mountain itself might be a god or the seat of a god; it might be a volcano, the home of the dread *Pele,* and into desert places few would venture but such as were adroit to snare the whispering spirits of the dead. Today, from the Wao Akua or the *Wao maʻu kele,* the gods perhaps have fled; the descendants of Vancouver's cattle fill them with less questionable terrors.

As we mounted the glacis of the island, the horses clattering on the lava, we saw far above us the curtain of the rain exclude the view. The sky was clear, the sun strong overhead; around us a thin growth of bushes and creepers glittered green in their black setting, like plants upon a ruinous pavement; all else was lava, wastes of lava, some of them enclosed (it seemed in wantonness) with dry stone walls. But the bushes, when the rain descends often enough from its residential altitude, flourish extremely; and cattle and asses, walking on these resonant slabs, collect a livelihood. Here and there a prickly pear came to the bigness of a standard tree and made a space of shade; under one I saw a donkey; under another no less than three cows huddled from the sun. Thus we had before our eyes the rationale of two of the native distinctions; traversed the zone of flowering shrubs; and saw above us the mist hang perennial in Ma'u.

As we continued to draw nearer to the rain, trees began to be mingled with the shrubs; and we came at last to where a house stood in an orchard of papayas, with their palmlike growth and collar of green gourds. In an outhouse stood the water barrel, that necessity of Kona life. For all the water comes from heaven, and must be caught and stored; and the name of Ho'okena itself may very well imply a cistern and a cup of water for the traveler along the coast. The house belonged to Nahinu, but was in occupation by an American, seeking to make butter there (if I understood) without success. The butter man was gone, to muse perhaps on fresh expeditions; his house was closed, and I was able to observe his three chambers only through the windows. In the first were milk pans and remains of breakfast; in the second, a bed; in the third, a scanty wardrobe hung from pegs, and two pirated novels lay on the floor. One was reversed and could not be identified; the name of the other I made out. It was *Little Lou.* Happy Mr. Clark Russell, making life pleasant for the exile in his garden of papayas, high over the sea, upon the forest edge, where the breeze comes freely.

A little way beyond we plunged into the forest. It grew at first very sparse and parklike, the trees of a pale verdure, but healthy, the parasites, *per contra,* often dead. Underfoot the ground was still a rockery of fractured lava; but now the interstices were filled with soil. A sedgelike grass (buffalo grass?) grew everywhere, and the horses munched it by the way, with relish. Candlenut trees with their white foliage stood in groves. Breadfruits were here and there, but never well to do; Hawaii is no true mother for the breadfruit or the coco palm. Mangoes, on the other hand, attained a splendid bigness, many of them discolored on one side with purplish hue, which struck the note of autumn. The same note was repeated by a certain aerial creeper, which drops, you might suppose, from heaven like the wreck of an old kite, and roosts on treetops with a pendant raffle of air roots, the whole of a color like a wintry beach's. These are clannish plants; five or six may be quartered on a single tree, thirty or forty on a grove; the wood dies under them to skeletons, and they swing there, like things hung out from washing, over the death they have provoked.

We had now turned southward toward Ka'a, following a shapeless bridle track which is the highroad of Hawaii. The sea was on one hand. Our way was across—the woods we threaded did but cling upon—

the vast declivity of the island front. For long, as we still skirted the margin of the forest, we kept an open view of the whole falling seaboard, the white edge of surf now soundless to our ears, and the high blue sea marbled by tide rips, and showing under the clouds of an opalescent milky white. The height, the breeze, the giddy gradient of the isle, delighted me. I observed a spider plant, its abhorred St. Andrew's cross against the sea and sky, certainly fifty yards from where I rode, and five feet at least from either tree; so wide was its death-gossamer spread, so huge the ugly vermin.

Presently the sea was lost, the forest swallowed us. Ferns joined their fronds above a horseman's head. High over these the dead and the living rose and were hung with tattered parasites. The breeze no longer reached us; it was steaming hot, and the way went up and down so abruptly that in one place my saddle girth was burst and we must halt for repairs. In the midst of this rough wilderness I was reminded of the aim of our excursion. The schoolmaster and certain others of Hoʻokena had recently bought a tract of land for some four thousand dollars, set out coffee, and hired a Chinaman to mind it. The thing was notable in itself; natives selling land is a thing of daily custom; of natives buying I have heard no other instance; and it was civil to show interest. "But when," I asked, "shall we come to your coffee plantation?" "This is it," said he, and pointed down. Their bushes grew on the path side; our horses breasted them as they went by, and the gray wood enclosed and overarched that thread of cultivation.

A little further we strung in single file through the

hot crypt, our horses munching grass, their riders chewing unpalatable gum collected from a tree. Next the wood opened, and we issued forth again into the day on the precipitous broadside of the isle. A village was before us, a Catholic church, and perhaps a dozen scattered houses, some of grass, in the old island fashion, others spick and span with outside stair and balcony and trellis and white paint and green, in the more modern taste. One arrested my attention; it stood on the immediate verge of a deep precipice, two stories high, with double balconies, painted white, and showing by my count fifteen windows. "There is a fine house," said I. "Outside," returned the schoolmaster dryly. "That is the way with natives; they spend money on the outside. Let us go there; you will find they live on the veranda, and have no furniture." We were made welcome, sure enough, on the veranda, and in the lower room, which I entered, there was not a chair or table; only mats on the floor and photographs and lithographs upon the wall. The house was an eidolon, designed to gladden the eye and enlarge the heart of the proprietor returning from Ho'okena, and its fifteen windows were only to be numbered from without. Doubtless that owner had attained his end, for I observed, when we were home again at Ho'okena, and Nahinu was describing our itinerary to his wife, he mentioned we had baited at *ka hale nui,* "the great house."

The photographs were of the royal family, that goes without saying in Hawaii; of the two lithographs, made in San Francisco, one I knew at first sight for General Garfield; the second tempted and tantalized me; it could not be, I thought—and yet it must; it was this dubiety which carried me across the threshold; and behold! it was indeed the Duke of Thunder [Lord Nelson, Duke of Brontë], his name printed under his effigies in the Hawaiianized form of "Nelesona." I thought it a fine instance of fame that his features and his empty sleeve should have been drawn on stone in San Francisco, which was a lone Mexican mission while he lived, and lettered for a market in those islands which were not yet united under Kamehameha when he died. And then I had a cold fit, and wondered after all if these good folk knew anything of the man's world-shaking deeds and gunpowder weaknesses, or if he was to them a "bare appellation" and a face on stone, and turning to the schoolmaster I asked of him the question. Yes, the Hawaiians knew of Nelesona; there had been a story in the papers where he figured, and the portrait had been given for a supplement. So he was known as a character of Romance! Brave men since Agamemnon, like the brave before, must patiently expect the "inspired author." And nowhere has fiction deeper roots than in the world of Polynesia. They are all tellers and hearers of tales, and the first requisite of any native paper is a story from the English or the French. These are of all sorts, and range from the works of good Miss Porter to *The Lightning Detective*. Miss Porter, I was told, was "drawing" in Hawaii; and Dumas and the *Arabian Nights* were named as having pleased extremely.

Our homeward way was down the hill and by the sea in the black open. We traversed a waste of shattered lava; spires, ravines; well-holes showing the entrance to vast subterranean vaults, in whose profundities our horses' hoofs doubtless echoed. The whole was clothed with stone florituri, fantastically fashioned, like debris from the workshop of some brutal sculptor; dogs' heads, devils, stone trees, and gargoyles broken in the making. From a distance, so intricate was the detail, the side of a hummock wore the appearance of some coarse and dingy sort of coral or a scorched growth of heather. Amid this jumbled wreck, naked itself and the evidence of old disaster, frequent plants found root; rose apples bore their rosy flowers, and a bush between a cypress and a juniper attained at times a height of twenty feet.

The breakneck path had descended almost to the sea, and we were already within sound of its reverberations, when a cliff hove up suddenly on the landward hand, very rugged and broken, streaked with white lichen, laddered with green lianas, and pierced with the apertures of half a hundred caves. Two of these were piously sealed with doors, the wood scarce withered. For the Hawaiian remembers the repository of the bones of old, and is still jealous of the safety of ancestral relics. Nor without cause. For the white man comes and goes upon the hunt for curiosities, and one (it is rumored) consults soothsayers and explores the caves of Kona after the fabled treasure of Kamehameha.

⚡3⚡

THE CITY OF REFUGE

Our way was northward on the naked lava. The sun smote us fair and full; the air streamed from the hot rock, the distant landscape gleamed and trembled through its vortices. On the left the coast heaved bodily upward to Maʻu, the zone of mists and forests, where it rains all day, and the clouds creep up and down, and the groves loom and vanish in the margin.

The land was still a crust of lava, here and there ramparted with cliffs, which here and there break down and show the mouths of branching galleries, mines, and tombs of nature's making, endlessly vaulted and ramified below our passage. Wherever a house is, coco palms spring sheer out of the rock; a little shabby in this northern latitude, not visibly the worse for their inclement rooting. Hoʻokena had shown out green under the black lip of the overhanging crag, green as a May orchard; the lava might have been some rich black loam. Everywhere, in the fissures of the rock, green herbs and flowering bushes

24

prospered; donkeys and cattle were everywhere, too, their whitened bones telling of drought. No sound but the sea pervades this region; and it smells strong of the open water and of aromatic plants.

We skirted one cliffy cove, full of bursting surges; and if it had not been for the palms, and the houses, and the canoes that were putting out to fish, and the color of the cliffs, and the bright dresses (lilac, red, and green) of the women that sat about the doors at work, I might have thought myself in Devonshire. A little further, we passed a garden enclosed in dry stone walls from the surrounding blackness; it seemed a wonder of fertility; hard by was the owner, a white man, waiting the turn of the tide by the margin of his well, so, soon as the sea flowed, he might begin to irrigate with brackish water. The children hailed my companion from wayside houses. With one little maid, knotting her gown about her in embarrassment so as to define her little person like a suit of tights, we held a conversation more prolonged. "Will you be at school tomorrow?" "Yes, sir." "Do you like school?" "Yes, sir." "Do you like bathing?" "No, ma'am," with a staggering change of sex. Another maiden, of more tender growth and wholly naked, fled into the house at our approach, and appeared again with a corner of a towel. Leaning one hand on the post, and applying her raiment with the other, she stood in the door and watched us haughtily by. The white flag of a surveyor and a poundmaster's notice on a board told of the reign of law.

At length we turned the corner of a point and debouched on a flat of lava. On the landward side, cliffs made a quadrant of an amphitheater, melting on either side into the general mountain of the isle. Over these, rivers of living lava had once flowed, had frozen as they fell, and now depended like a sculptured drapery. Here and there the mouth of a cave was seen half blocked, some green lianas beckoning in the entrance. In front, the fissured pavement of the lava stretched into the sea and made a surfy point. A scattered village, two white churches, one Catholic, one Protestant, a grove of tall and scraggy palms, and a long bulk of ruin occupy the end. Off the point, not a cable's length beyond the breaching surf, a schooner rode; come to discharge house boards, and presently due at Ho'okena to load lepers. The village is Hōnaunau; the ruin, the Hale o Keawe, temple and city of refuge.

The ruin made a massive figure, rising from the flat lava in ramparts twelve to fifteen feet high, of an equal thickness, and enclosing an area of several acres. The unmortared stones were justly set; in places the bulwark was still true to the plummet, in places ruinous from the shock of earthquakes. The enclosure was divided in unequal parts; the greater, the city of refuge; the smaller, the heiau or temple, the so-called House of Keawe, or reliquary of his royal bones. Not his alone, but those of many monarchs of Hawaii were treasured here; but whether as the founder of the shrine or because he had been more renowned in life, Keawe was the naming and the hallowing saint. And Keawe can produce at least one claim to figure on the canon, for since his death he has wrought miracles. As late as 1829 Ka'ahumanu sent messengers to bring the relics of the kings from their long repose at Hōnaunau. First to the keeper's wife and then to the keeper the spirit of Keawe appeared in a dream, bidding them prevent the desecration. Upon the second summons they rose trembling; hasted with a torch into the crypt; exchanged the bones of Keawe with those of some less holy chieftains; and were back in bed but not yet asleep, and the day had not yet dawned before the messengers arrived. So it comes that to this hour the bones of Keawe, like those of his descendant, sleep in some unknown crevice of that caverned isle.

When Ellis passed in 1823, six years before this intervention of the dead, the temple still preserved some shadow of its ancient credit and presented much of its original appearance. He has sketched it, rudely in a drawing, more effectively in words. "Several rudely carved male and female images of wood were placed on the outside of the enclosure: some on low pedestals under the shade of an adjacent tree, others on high posts on the jutting rocks that hung over the edge of the water. A number stood on the fence at unequal distances all around, but the principal assemblage of these frightful representatives of their former deities was at the southeast end of the enclosed space where, forming a semicircle, twelve of them stood in grim array, as if perpetual guardians of 'the mighty dead' reposing in the house adjoining. Once they had evidently been clothed, but now they appeared in the most indigent nakedness. The horrid stare of these idols, the tattered garments upon some of them, and the heaps of rotting offerings before them, seemed to us no improper emblems of the system they were designed to support; distinguished alike by its cruelty, folly, and wretchedness. We endeavored to gain admission to the inside of the house, but were told it was strictly prohibited. However, by pushing one of the boards across the doorway a little on one side, we looked in and saw many large images, with distended mouths, large rows of shark's teeth, and pearl-shell eyes. We also saw several bundles, apparently of human bones, cleaned, carefully tied up with sennit made of coconut fiber, and placed in different parts of the house, together with some rich shawls and other valuable articles, probably worn by those to whom the bones belonged." Thus the careless eyes of Ellis viewed and passed over the bones of sacrosanct Keawe, in his house which he had builded.

Cities of refuge are found not only in Hawaii, but in the Gilberts, where their name is now invariably used for a mosquito net. But the refuge of the Gilberts was only a house in a village, and only offered, like European churches, a sanctuary for the time. The hunted man might harbor there and live on charity; woe to him if he stepped without. The city of refuge of Hōnaunau possessed a larger efficacy. Its gate once passed, an appearance made before the priest on duty, a hasty prayer addressed to the chief idol, and the guilty man was free to go again, relieved from all the consequences of his crime or his misfortune. In time of war its bulwarks were advertised by pennons of white tapa; and the aged, the children, and the poorer hearted of the women of the district awaited there the issue of the battle. But the true wives followed their lords into the field and shared with them their toil and danger.

The city had yet another function. There was in Hawaii a class apart, comparable to the doomed families of Tahiti, whose special mission was to supply the altar. It seems that the victim fell usually on the holy day, of which there were four in the month; between these, the man was not only safe but enjoyed, in virtue of his destiny, a singular license of behavior. His immunities exceeded those of the medieval priest and jester rolled in one; he might have donned the King's girdle (the height of sacrilege and treason) and gone abroad with it, unpunished and apparently unblamed; and with a little care and some acquaintance in priests' families, he might prolong this life of license to old age. But the laws of human nature are implacable; their destiny of privilege and peril turned the men's heads; even at dangerous seasons they went recklessly abroad upon their pleasures; were often sighted in the open, and must run for the city of refuge with the priestly murderers at their heels. It is strange to think that it was a priest, also, who stood in the door to welcome and protect them.

The enclosure of the sanctuary was all paved with lava; scattered blocks encumbered it in places; everywhere tall coco palms jutted from the fissures and drew shadows on the floor; a loud continuous sound of the near sea burdened the ear. These rude monumental ruins, and the thought of that life and death of which they stood memorial, threw me in a muse. There are times and places where the past becomes more vivid than the present, and the memory dominates the ear and eye. I have found it so in the presence of the vestiges of Rome; I found it so again in the city of refuge at Hōnaunau; and the strange, busy, and perilous existence of the old Hawaiian, the grinning idols of the heiau, the priestly murderers and the fleeting victim, rose before and mastered my imagination.

Some dozen natives of Hōnaunau followed me about to show the boundaries; and I was recalled from these thoughts by one of my guides laying his hand on a big block of lava.

"This stone is called Ka'ahumanu," said he. "It is here she lay hid with her dog from Kamehameha."

And he told me an anecdote, which would not interest the reader as it interested me, until he has learned what manner of woman Ka'ahumanu was.

☙ 4 ❧

KAʻAHUMANU

Kamehameha the First, founder of the realm of the Eight Islands, was a man properly entitled to the style of Great. All chiefs in Polynesia are tall and portly, and Kamehameha owed his life in the battle with the Puna fishers to the vigor of his body. He was skilled in single combat; as a general, he was almost invariably the victor. Yet it is not as a soldier that he remains fixed upon the memory; rather as a kindly and wise monarch, full of sense and shrewdness, like an old, plain, country farmer. When he had a mind to make a present of fish, he went to the fishing himself. When famine fell on the land he remitted the tributes; cultivated a garden for his own support with his own hands, and set all his friends to do the like. These patches of land, each still known by the name of its high-born gardener, were shown to Ellis on his tour. He passed laws against cutting down young sandalwood trees and against the killing of the bird from which the feather mantles of the archipelago were made. The yellow feathers were to be plucked, he directed, and the bird dismissed again to freedom. His people were astonished. "You are old," they argued, "soon you will die; what use will it be to you?" "Let the bird go," said the King. "It will be for my children afterward." Alas, that this law had not prevailed! Sandalwood and yellow feathers are things of yesterday in his dominions.

The attitude of this brave old fellow to the native religion was, for some while before his death, ambiguous. A white man (tradition says) had come to Hawaii upon a visit. King Kalākaua assures me he was an Englishman and a missionary [John Howel, former Church of England clergyman]. If that be so, he should be easy to identify. It was this missionary's habit to go walking in the morning ere the sun was up, and, before doing so, to kindle a light and make tea. The King, who rose early himself to watch the behavior of his people, observed the light, made inquiries, learned of and grew curious about these morning walks, threw himself at last in the missionary's path, and drew him into talk. The meeting was repeated, and the missionary began to press the King with Christianity. "If you will throw yourself from that cliff," said Kamehameha, "and come down uninjured, I will accept your religion; not unless." But the missionary was a man of parts. He wrought a deep impression on his hearer's mind, and after he had left for home Kamehameha called his chief priest, and announced that he was about to break the tabus and to change his faith. The kahuna replied that he was the King's servant, but the step was grave, and it would be wiser to proceed by divination. Kamehameha consented. Each built a new heiau over against the other's, and when both were finished a game of what we call French and English, or the tug-of-war, was played upon the intervening space. The party of the priest prevailed; the King's men were dragged in a body into the opposite temple, and the tabus were maintained. None employed in this momentous foolery was informed of its significance; the King's misgivings were studiously concealed; but there is little doubt he continued to cherish them in secret. At his death he had another memorable word, testifying to his old preoccupation for his son's estate, implying, besides, a weakened confidence in the island deities. His sickness was heavy upon him; the time had manifestly come to offer sacrifice; the people had fled already from the dangerous vicinity and lay hid; none but priests and chiefs remained about the King. "A man to your god!" they argued; "a man to your god that you may recover!" "The man is sacred to my son the King," replied Kamehameha. So much appeared in public; but it is believed that he left secret commands upon the high chief Kalanimoku, and on Ka'ahumanu, the most beautiful and energetic of his wives, to do, as soon as he was dead, that which he had spared to do while living.

No time was lost. The very day of his death, May 8, 1819, the women of the court ate of forbidden food, and some of the men sat down with them to eat. Infidelity must have been deep-seated in the circle of Kamehameha, for no portent followed this defiance of the gods, and none of the transgressors died. But the priests doubtless were informed of what was doing; the blame lay clearly on the shoulders of Ka'ahumanu, the most conspicuous person in the land, named by the dying Kamehameha for a conditional successor: "If Liholiho do amiss, let Ka'ahumanu take the kingdom and preserve it." The priests met in council of diviners, and by a natural retort it was upon Ka'ahumanu that they laid the fault of the King's death. This conspiracy appears to have been quite in vain. Ka'ahumanu sat secure. On the day of the coronation, when the young King came forth from the heiau, clad in a red robe and crowned with his English diadem, it was almost as an equal that she met and spoke to him. "Son of heaven, I name to you the possession of your father; here are the chiefs, there are the people of your father; there are your guns, here is your land. But let you and me enjoy that land together." He must have known already she was a free-eater, and there is no doubt he trembled at the thought of that impiety and its punishment; yet he consented to what seems her bold proposal. The same day he met his own mother, who signed to him privately that he should eat free. But Liholiho (the poor drunkard who died in London) was incapable of so much daring; he hung long apart from the court circle with a clique of the more superstitious, and it was not till five months later, after a drinking bout in a canoe at sea, that he was decoyed to land by stronger spirits, and was seen (perhaps scarce conscious of his acts) to eat of a dog, drink rum, and smoke tobacco with his servant women. Thus the food tabu fell finally at court. Ere it could be stamped out upon Hawaii a war must be fought, wherein the chief of the old party fell in battle, his brave wife Manono by his side, mourned even by the missionary Ellis.

The fall of one tabu involved the fall of others; the land was plunged in dissolution; morals ceased. When the missionaries came (in April 1820) all the wisdom in the kingdom was prepared to embrace the succor of some new idea.

Ka'ahumanu early ranged upon that side, perhaps at first upon a ground of politics. But gradually she fell more and more under the influence of the new teachers; loved them, served them; valorously defended them in dangers, which she shared, and put away at their command her second husband. To the end of a long life she played an almost sovereign part, so that in the ephemerides of Hawaii the progresses of Ka'ahumanu are chronicled along with the deaths and the accessions of Kings. For two successive sovereigns and in troublous periods she held the reins of regency with a fortitude that has not been called in question, with a loyalty beyond reproach, and at last, on the 5th of June 1832, this Duke of Wellington of a woman made the end of a saint, fifty-seven years after her marriage with the conqueror. The date of her birth, it seems, is lost. We may call her seventy.

Ka'ahumanu was a woman of the chiefly stature and of celebrated beauty: Bingham admits she was "beautiful for a Polynesian," and her husband cherished her exceedingly. He had the indelicacy to frame and publish an especial law declaring death against the man who should approach her, and yet no penalty against herself. And in 1809, after thirty-four years of marriage and when she must have been nearing fifty, an island Chastelard of the name of Kanihonui was found to be her lover and paid the penalty of life, she cynically surviving. Some twenty years later one of the missionaries had written home denouncing the misconduct of an English whaler. The whaler got word of the denunciation and, with the complicity of the English consul, sought to make a crime of it against the mission. Party spirit ran very violent in the islands, tears were shed, threats flying, and Ka'ahumanu called a council of the chiefs. In that day stood forth the native historian, David Malo (though his name should rather have been Nathan), and pressed the regent with historic instances. Who was to be punished? The whaler guilty of the act, the missionary whose denunciation had provoked the scandal? "Oh, you, the wife of Kamehameha," said he. "Kanihonui came and slept with you; Luheluhe declared to Kamehameha the sleeping together of you two. I ask you which of these two persons was slain by Kamehameha? Was it Luheluhe?" And she answered, "It was Kanihonui!" Shakespeare never imagined such a character; and it would require none less than he to represent her sublimities and contradictions.

After this heroine the stone in the precinct of Hōnaunau had been named. Here is the reason, and the tale completes her portrait. Kamehameha was, of course, polygamous; the number of his wives rose at last to twenty-five; and out of these no less than two were the sisters of Ka'ahumanu. The favorite was of a jealous habit; and when it came to a sister for a rival her jealousy overflowed. She fled by night, plunged in the sea, came swimming to Hōnaunau, entered the precinct by the sea gate, and hid herself behind the stone. There she lay naked and refused food. The flight was discovered; as she had come swimming, none had seen her pass; the priests of the temple were bound, it seems, to silence, and Kona was filled with the messengers of the dismayed Kamehameha vainly seeking the favorite. Now Ka'ahumanu had a dog who was much attached to her, who had accompanied her in her long swim, and lay by her side behind the stone; and it chanced, as the messengers ran past the city of refuge, that the dog (perhaps recognizing them) began to bark. "Ah, there is the dog of Ka'ahumanu!" said the messengers, and returned and told the King she was at the Hale o Keawe. Thence Kamehameha fetched or sent for her, and the breach in their relations was restored.

A King preferred this woman out of a kingdom; Kanihonui died for her when she was fifty; even her dog adored her; even Bingham, who did not see her until 1820, thought her "beautiful for a Polynesian"; and while she was thus in person an emblem of womanly charm, she made her life illustrious with the manly virtues. There are some who give to Mary, Queen of Scots, the place of saint, and muse in their historic meditations; I recommend to them instead the wife and widow of the island conqueror. The Hawaiian was the nobler woman, with the nobler story; and no disenchanting portrait will be found to shatter an ideal.

☙ 5 ☙

THE LEPERS OF KONA

A step beyond Hoʻokena a wooden house with two doors stands isolated in a field of broken lava, like plowed land. I had approached it on the night of my arrival and found it black and silent; yet even then it had inmates. A man and a woman sat there captive, and the man had a knife, brought to him in secret by his family. Not long, perhaps, after I was by, the man, silencing by threats his fellow prisoner, cut through the floor and escaped to the mountain. It was known he had a comrade there, hunted on the same account; and their friends kept them supplied with food and ammunition. Upon the mountains, in most islands of the group, similar outlaws rove in bands or dwell alone, unsightly hermits; and but the other day an officer was wounded while attempting an arrest. Some are desperate fellows; some mournful women—mothers and wives; some stripling girls. For instance, a day or two after the man escaped the police got word of another old offender, made a forced march, and took the quarry sitting, this time with little peril to themselves. For the out-law was a girl of nineteen, who had been two years under the rains in the high forest, with her mother for comrade and accomplice. How does their own poet sing?

> In the land of distress
> My dwelling was on the mountain height,
> My talking companions were the birds,
> The decaying leaves of the ki my clothing.

It is for no crime this law-abiding race flee to the woods; it is no fear for the gallows or the dungeon that nerves themselves to resist and their friends to aid and to applaud them. Their liability is for disease; they are lepers, and what they combine to combat is not punishment, but segregation. While China and England and France, in their tropical possessions, either attempt nothing or effect little, Hawaii has honorably faced the problem of this ancient and apparently reviving malady. Her small extent is an advantage; but the ruggedness of the physical character, the desert woods and mountains, and the habit of the native mind oppose success. To the native mind, our medical opinions seem unfounded. We smile to hear of ghosts and gods; they smile when told to keep warm in fevers or to avoid contagion. Leprosy in particular they cannot be persuaded to avoid. But no mere opinion would exalt them to resist the law and lie in forests did not a question of the family bond embitter and exasperate the opposition.

Their family affection is strong, but unerect; it is luxuriously self-indulgent, circumscribed within the passing moment, without providence, without nobil-

ity, incapable of healthful rigor. The presence and
the approval of the loved one, it matters not how
purchased, there is the single demand of the Polynesian. By a natural consequence, when death inter-
venes, he is consoled the more easily.

Against this undignified fervor of attachment, mar-
ital and parental, the law of segregation often beats
in vain. It is no fear of the Lazaretto; they know the
dwellers are used well in Molokai; they receive letters from friends already there who praise the place,
and, could the family be taken in a body, they would
go with glee, overjoyed to draw rations from government. But all cannot become pensioners at once, a
proportion of ratepayers must be kept; and the leper
must go alone, or with a single relative; and the native instinctively resists the separation as a weasel
bites. A similar reluctance can be shown in Molokai
itself. By a recent law, clean children born within
the precinct are taken from their leper parents, sent
to an intermediate hospital, and given a chance of
life and health and liberty. I have stood by while Mr.
Meyer and Mr. Hutchinson, the luna [overseer] and
the subluna of the Lazaretto, opened the petitions of
the settlement. As they sat together on the steps of
the guesthouse at Kalawao, letter after letter was
passed between them with a sneer and flung upon
the ground, till I was at last struck with their cavalier
procedure, and inquired the nature of the appeals.
They were all the same; all from leper parents, all
pleading to have their clean children retained in
that abode of sorrow, and all alleging the same reason—*aloha nui nui*—an extreme affection. Such was
the extreme affection of Ka'ahumanu for Kanihonui,

by which she indulged her wantonness in safety and he died. But love was a countenance more severe.

The scenes I am about to describe, moving as they were to witness, have thus an element of something weak and false. Sympathy may flow freely for the leper girl; it may flow for her mother with reserve; it must not betray us into injustice for the government whose laws they had attempted to evade.

I walked in a bright sun, after a grateful rain, upon the shore beyond Hoʻokena. The breeze was of heavenly freshness, the surf was jubilant in all the caves; it was a morning to put a man in thought of the antiquity, the health, and cleanness of the earth. And behold! when I came abreast of the little pest-house on the lava both the doors were open. In front a circle of some half a dozen women and children sat conspicuous in the usual bright raiment; in their midst was a crouching and bowed figure, swathed in a black shawl and motionless; and as I drew more near I was aware of a continuous and high-pitched drone of song. The figure in the midst was the leper girl; the song was the improvisation of the mother, pouring out her sorrow in the island way. "That was not singing," explained the schoolmaster's wife on my return, "that was crying!" And she sketched for me the probable tenor of the lament: "Oh, my daughter! Oh, my daughter, now you are going away from me, now you are taken away from me at last," and so on without end.

The thought of the girl separated so early from her fellows—the look of her there covered from eyesight, like an untimely birth—perhaps more than all, the penetrating note of the lament—subdued my courage utterly. With the natural impulse, I began to seek some outlet for my pain. It occurred to me that after two years in the woods the family affairs might well have suffered, and in view of the transplantation, clothes, furniture, or money might be needful. I believe it was not done wisely, since it was gone about in ignorance; I dare say it flowed from a sentiment no more erect than that of Polynesians. I am sure there were many in England to whom my superfluity had proved more useful; but the next morning saw me at the pesthouse, under convoy of the schoolmaster and the policeman.

The doors were again open. A fire was burning and a pot cooking on the lava, under the supervision of an old woman in a grass-green sacque. This dame, who seemed more merry than refined, hailed me, seized me, and tried to seat me in her lap; a jolly and coarse old girl from whom, in my hour of sentiment, I fled with craven shrinking; to whom, upon a retrospect, I do more justice. The two lepers, both women, sat in the midst of their visitors, even the children, to my grief, touching them freely; the elder chatting at intervals—the girl in the same black weed and bowed in the same attitude as yesterday. It was painfully plain she would conceal, if possible, her face.

Perhaps she had been beautiful; certainly, poor soul, she had been vain—a gift of equal value. Some consultation followed: I was told that nothing was required for outfit, but a gift in money would be gratefully received; and this, forgetting I was in the South Seas, I was about to make in silence. The confounded expression of the schoolmaster reminded me of where I was. We stood up, accordingly, side by side before the lepers; I made the necessary speech, which the schoolmaster translated sentence by sentence; the money, thus hallowed by oratory, was handed over and received: and the two women each returned a dry *"Mahalo,"* the girl not even then exhibiting her face.

Between 9 and 10 of the same morning the schooner lay to off Ho'okena and a whaleboat came ashore. The village clustered on the rocks for the farewell; a grief perhaps—a performance certainly. We miss in our modern life these operatic consolations of the past. The lepers came singly and unattended, the elder first, the girl a little after, tricked out in a red dress and with a fine red feather in her hat. In this bravery, it was the more affecting to see her move apart on the rocks and crouch in her accustomed attitude. But this time I had seen her face: it was scarce horribly affected, but had a haunting look of an unfinished wood doll, at once expressionless and disproportioned; doubtless a sore spectacle in the mirror of youth. Next there appeared a woman of the middle life, of a swaggering gait, a gallant figure, and a bold, handsome face. She came, swinging her hat, rolling her eyes and shoulders, visibly working herself up; the crowd stirred and murmured on her passage; and I knew without being told this was the mother and protagonist. Close by the sea, in the midst of the spectators, she sat down, and raised immediately the notes of the lament. One after another of her friends approached her. To one after the other she reached out an arm, embraced them down, rocked awhile with them embraced, and passionately kissed them in the island fashion, with the pressed face.

The leper girl at last, as at some signal, rose from her seat apart, drew near, was inarmed like the rest, and with a small knot (I suppose of the most intimate) held some while in a general clasp. Through all the wail continued, rising into words and a sort of passionate declamatory recitation as each friend approached, sinking again as the pair rocked together into the tremolo drone. At length the scene was over; the performers rose; the lepers and the mother were helped in silence to their places; the whaleboat was urged between the reefs into a bursting surge, and swung next moment without on the smooth swell. Almost every countenance about me streamed with tears.

It was odd, but perhaps natural among a ceremonious, oratorical race, that the boat should have waited while a passenger publicly lamented on the beach. It was more odd, still, that the mother should have been the chief, rather the only actor. She was leaving indeed; she hoped to be taken as a *kokua,* or clean assistant, and thus accompany her daughter to the settlement; but she was far from sure, and it was highly possible she might return to Kona in a month. The lepers, on the other hand, took leave forever. Insofar as regarded their own isle and birthplace, and for their friends and families, it was their day of death.

> The soldier from the war returns,
> The sailor from the main;
> But not the sick from the gray island.

Yet they went unheeded, and the chief part, and the whole stage and sympathy was for their traveling companion.

THE EIGHT ISLANDS

At the time I was too deeply moved to criticize; mere sympathy oppressed my spirit. It had always been a point with me to visit the station if I could; on the rocks of Hoʻokena the design was fixed. I had seen the departure of lepers for the place of exile; I must see their arrival and that place itself.

❧ 6 ❧

THE LAZARETTO

The windward coast of Molokai is gloomy and abrupt. A wall of cliff of from two to three thousand feet in height extends the more part of the length (some forty miles) from east to west. Wood clusters on its front like ivy; and in the wet season streams descend in waterfalls and play below on the surface of the ocean. For in almost the whole of its length the cliff, without the formality of any beach, plunges in the Pacific. Bold water follows the coast; ships may almost everywhere approach within a trifling distance of the towering shore; and immediately in front of Molokai surveyors have found some of the deepest soundings of that ocean. This unusual depth of water, the continuity of the trade [winds] and the length of which fetch extends unbroken from the shores of California, magnify the sea. The swell is nursed by the steady wind, it grows in that long distance, it draws near through the deep soundings without combing, and spends itself undiminished on the cliffs of Molokai.

THE EIGHT ISLANDS

Toward the eastern end a river in a winding glen descends from the interior; the barrier is quite broken here, and a beach is formed and makes a place of call, Wailau. A few miles farther east, the cove of Pelekunu offers a doubtful chance of landing, and is also visited by steamers. The third and last place of approach is at the Lazaretto. A shelf of undercliff here borders the precipice, expanding toward its western end in a blunt promontory, a little more than a mile square. The lee of this precipice offers unusual facilities for landing and, in favorable states of wind and sea, ships may anchor. But these facilities to seaward are more than counterbalanced by the uncompromising character of the barrier behind. The pali (as the precipice is called) in the extent of this strip of undercliff makes three recesses, Waihanau, Waialeia, and Waikolu—as their names imply, three gutters of the mountain. These are clothed in wood; from a distance they show like verdant niches and retreats for lovers; but the face of the rock is so precipitous that only in the first, Waihanau, is there a practicable path. The rains continually destroy it; it must be renewed continually; to ride there is impossible; to mount without frequent falls seems unexpected; and even the descent exhausts a powerful man. The existence of another path more to the westward was affirmed to me by some, denied by others. At the most, therefore, in two points, the cliff is scantly passable upward. Passage coastwise is beyond expectation to any creature without wings. To the west, the strip of undercliff simply discontinues. To the east, the wall itself thrusts forth a huge protrusion, and the way is barred except to fish and seabirds. Here, then, is a prison fortified by nature, a place where thousands may be quartered and a pair of sentinels suffice to watch and hold the only issues.

The undercliff is in itself narrow; it is widened on one hand by the recesses of the cliff, and on the other by the expansion of the foreland; and the last contains (for a guess) two-thirds of the whole territory. It rises in the midst to a low hill enclosing a dead crater, like a quarry hole; the interior sides clothed with trees; at the foot a salt pool, unsoundable, at least unsounded. Hence the land slopes to the sea's edge and upward toward the pali in grassy downs. A single sick pandanus breaks, or broke while I was there, that naked heath; except in man's enclosures, I can recall nowhere else one switch of timber. The foreland is grazed by some fifteen hundred head of stock, seven hundred of them horses, for the patients are continual and furious riders; the rest cows and asses. These all do excellently well. The horrid pest to which the place is sacred spares them, being man's prerogative. It was strange to see those droves of animals feeding and sporting in exuberant health by the sea margin, and to reflect upon their destiny, brought from so far, at so much cost and toil, only to be ridden to and fro upon and eaten by the defeatured and dying.

The shaven down, the scattered boulders, the cry of the wind in the grass, the frequent showers of rain, the bulk of the pali, the beating of the near sea, all the features and conditions strike the mind as northern, and to the northerner the scene is in consequence grateful, like one of his native minor tunes. It is stirring to look eastward and see the huge viridescent mountain front sunder the settlement from the next habitations of clean men at Pelekunu—at its foot, in the sea, two tilted islets. It is pleasant in the early morning to ride by the roots of the pali, when the low sun and the cool breeze are in your face, and from above, in the cliffside forest, falls a perpetual chirruping of birds. It is pleasant, above all, to wander by the margin of the sea. The heath breaks down, like Helicon, in cliffs. A narrow fringe of emerald edges the precipitous shore; close beyond the blue shows the bold soundings; the wanderer stands plainly on a mere buttress of the vast cathedral front of the island, and above and below him, in the air and in the water, the precipice continues. Along the brink, rock architecture and sea music please the senses, and in that tainted place the thought of the cleanness of the antiseptic ocean is welcome to the mind.

Yet this is but one side of the scenery of the Lazaretto: and I received an impression strongly contrasted when I entered the recess of Waialeia. The sides were niched and channeled with dry tracks of torrents, grass clung on the sheer precipice, forest clustered on the smallest vantage of a shelf. The floor of the amphitheater was piled with shattered rock, detritus of the mountain, with which, in the time of the rains, the torrents had maintained a cannonade. Vigorously black themselves, these were spotted with snow-white lichen and shaded and intermingled with plants and trees of a vivid green. The day was overcast; clouds ran low about the edges of the basin; and yet the colors glowed as though immersed in sunshine. On the downs the effect is of some bleak, noble coast of Scotland or Scandinavia; here in the recess I felt myself transported to the tropics.

There are two villages, Kalaupapa, on the western shore of the promontory, Kalawao, toward the east upon the strip of undercliff; and along the road which joins them, each reaches forth scattered habitations.

Kalaupapa, the most sheltered in prevailing winds, is the customary landing place. When the run of the sea inclines the other way, ships pass far to the eastward near the two islets, and passengers are landed with extreme difficulty, and I was assured, not without danger, on a spur of rock. Kalaupapa, being quite upon the downs, is the more bleak; a long, bare, irregular, ungardened village of unsightly houses. Here are two churches, Protestant and Catholic, and the Bishop Home for Girls. Kalawao is even beautiful; pleasant houses stand in gardens of flowers; the pali rises behind; in front, across the sea, the eye commands the islets and the huge green face of cliff excluding Pelekunu. This is the view from the window of the lay brother, Mr. Dutton, and he assured me he found its beauty far more striking than the deformations of the sick. The passing visitor can scarce attain to such philosophy. Here is Damien's Home for Boys. Close behind is a double graveyard, where some of the dead retain courtesy titles, and figure in their epitaphs as "Mr." or as "Mrs." The inevitable twin churches complete the village. A fifth church, the church of the Mormons, exists somewhere in the settlement; but I could never find it. On the westward end of Kalawao what we may call the official quarter stretches toward the promontory.

THE EIGHT ISLANDS

The main feature is the enclosure of the hospital and prison, where bad cases and bad characters are kept in surveillance; a green in a stockade with a few papayas and one flowering oleander, surrounded on three sides by low white houses. A little way off, enclosed in walls and hedges, stands the guesthouse of Kalawao, and, beyond that again, the quarters of the doctor.

The guesthouse is kept ready for the visits of members of the board. I arrived there early in the day, opened the gate, turned my horse loose, and entered in possession of the vacant house. I wandered through its chambers, visited the bathroom and the kitchen, and at last, throwing myself upon a bed, I fell asleep. Not before the hour of dinner, Dr. Swift, returning from his duties, wakened me and introduced himself. A similar arrival may be read of in the tale of the Three Bears; and that is well called a guesthouse where there is no host. Singular indeed is the isolation of the visitor in the Lazaretto. No patient is suffered to approach his place of residence. His room is tidied out by a clean helper during the day and while he is abroad. He returns at night to solitary walls. For a while a bell sounds at intervals from the hospital; silence succeeds, only pointed by the humming of the surf or the chirp of crickets. He steps to his door; perhaps a light still shines in the hospital; all else is dark. He returns and sits by his lamp and the crowding experiences besiege his memory; sights of pain in a land of disease and disfigurement, bright examples of fortitude and kindness, moral beauty, physical horror, intimately knit. He must be a man very little impressionable if he recall not these hours with an especial poignancy; he must be a man either very virtuous or very dull, if they were not hours of self-review and vain aspirations after good.

When the Hawaiian Government embraced the plan of segregation they were doubtless (as is the way of governments) unprepared, and the constitution of the Lazaretto, as it now exists, was approached by blunder and reached by accident. There was no design to pauperize; the lepers were to work, and in whole or part be self-supporting; and when a site fell to be chosen, some extent of cultivable soil was first required. In this, as in other conditions, Kalawao was wholly fitted for the purpose. In the old days, when Molokai swarmed with population, the foreland must have been a busy and perhaps a holy place; and thirty years ago it was covered with the ruins of heiaus, but still inhabited and still in active cultivation. Terms of sale were easily agreed upon. Unhappily, the government coquetted; the farmers were held for months under suspense; for months, in consequence, their houses were left unrepaired, their fields untilled; and the property was already much deteriorated before the purchase was confirmed and the clean inhabitants ejected from the foreland. The history of misgovernment by board followed the common course to the customary end; *too late* was coupled as usual with *too early;* the government had procrastinated to its loss, yet even then it was unready, and for another period of months the deserted farms lay idle. At length the first shipment of lepers landed (1865) with a small kit of blankets, tin dishes, and the like, but neither food nor money, to find the roofs fallen from the houses and the taro rotting in the ground.

They were strangers to each other, collected by common calamity, disfigured, mortally sick, banished without sin from home and friends. Few would understand the principle on which they were thus forfeited in all that makes life dear; many must have conceived their ostracism to be grounded in malevolent caprice; all came with sorrow at heart, many with despair and rage. In the chronicle of man there is perhaps no more melancholy landing than this of the leper immigrants among the ruined houses and dead harvests of Molokai. But the spirit of our race is finely tempered and the business of life engrossing to the last. As the spider, when you have wrecked its web, begins immediately to spin fresh strands, so these exiles, widowed, orphaned, unchilded, legally dead and physically dying, struck root in their new place. By a culpable neglect in the authorities they were suffered to divide among themselves the whole territory of the settlement; fell to work with growing hope, repaired the houses, replanted the fields, and began to look about them with the pride of the proprietor. Upon this scene of reviving industry a second deportation arrived, and the first were called upon to share and subdivide their lots. They did so, not without complaint, which the authorities disregarded; a third shipment followed shortly after in the same conditions, and a further redistribution of the land was imposed upon the early settlers. Remuneration was demanded; government demurred upon the price; the lepers were affronted, withdrew their offer, and stood upon their rights, and a new regimen arose of necessity. The two first companies continued to subsist upon their farms; but the third, and all subsequent shipments, must be fed by government. Pauperism had begun, and the original design miscarried. Today all are paupers; the single occasion of healthy interest and exercise subducted, and the country at large saddled with the support of many useless mouths.

THE LAZARETTO—*Continued*

The lepers, cast out from society and progressively deprived of employment, swiftly de-
civilized. *"Aole kānāwai ma keia wahi!"*—"There is
no law in this place"—was their word of salutation
to newcomers; cards, dancing, and debauch were the
diversions; the women served as prostitutes, the children as drudges; the dying were callously uncared
for; heathenism revived; okolehao [alcoholic liquor
distilled from ti or taro roots] was brewed, and in
their orgies the disfigured sick ran naked by the sea.
This is Damien's picture; these traits were viewed
through the tarnish of missionary spectacles; but they
seem all true to the human character in that unnatural
and gloomy situation, nor is there one that need surprise a student of his fellow men. What may, indeed,
surprise him—and what Damien, true to the clerical
prevention, neglected to commemorate—is the lack
of crime. Since 1865, the year of the landing, blood
has been shed but once in the precinct; and the chief
difficulty felt by successive rulers has been one in-

evitable in a colony of paupers, that of administration.

There has been but one chief luna from the first—Mr. Meyer, a man of much sagacity and force of character. But Mr. Meyer dwells in his own house on the top of the pali; comes to the settlement only at fixed intervals or upon some emergency, and even then approaches it with precautions, which I could not but admire, and to which, in all likelihood, he owes his long immunity from the disease. He may thus be rather regarded as a visiting inspector, and the subluna resident among the lepers and most frequently a leper himself, as the proper ruler of Kalawao. No less than ten persons have held this post in little more than twenty years, a fact which gives a measure at once of the difficulty of the office and the brevity of leper life.

The first was a Frenchman of the name of Lepart, a capable, high-spirited man; he was calumniated to the government, justified himself, and resigned. A British officer of the name of Walsh succeeded, soon died, and on his deathbed prayed to have the office continued to his wife. As this lady suffered from some deficiency of sight, and spoke no Hawaiian, there was conjoined with her an old ship captain, "a rough, honest, bawling good fellow," as ignorant of Hawaiian as herself. This unpromising ministry fell at last, not by its own weakness, but the fault of others. The Board of Health was already giving a ration of butcher's meat, so many pounds a week to every patient; and the Ministry of the Interior, alarmed at the growing expense, issued an order limiting the number of cattle to be slaughtered.

The figures were inconsistent; Mrs. Walsh quite properly obeyed the last command; the ration was in consequence reduced, and the lepers, under the lead of an able half-white, took out more cattle and killed them for themselves. A ship with police was despatched from Honolulu to quell this horrid rising; the half-white was imprisoned, and Mrs. Walsh and the skipper removed. A full-blood Hawaiian, who had been captain of the King's guard, was chosen to succeed. He was a good man, a very bad luna; stood in fear of every one; always supposed he should be "prayed to death," and did, in fact, whether from the result of enchantments or the fear of them, die within the year. The next appointment was equally daring and successful. The ablest man in the Lazaretto, the half-white who had killed the cattle, was installed as ruler—from the prison to the throne. He was one of those who must either rule or rebel, and as soon as he held the chief place and till death removed him the settlement was quiet.

Another half-white followed, the famous Billy Ragsdale, who had left a broad mark on the traditions of the colony. They tell that he sat in his porch and suitors approached him on their knees; that he sent his glove to the store or the butcher's for a token, and that Mrs. Ragsdale went to church on Sunday with two boys bearing her train and a third holding her umbrella. Mr. Meyer (I am aware) denies these scandals; he might have been the last to hear of them, had they existed, and man, though he delights in making myths, is usually inspired by some original in fact. That Ragsdale was arrogant is, besides, undoubted, for his arrogance came near plunging the settlement in war. Hawaiians readily obey a half-white, still more readily a man of chiefly caste. Now there lived in the settlement, in Ragsdale's day, a brother of Queen Emma, Prince Peter Kaiu [Kaeo]. Of a sudden Mr. Meyer received (by a messenger coming breathless up the pali) a curt, civil, menacing note from Prince Peter. If Ragsdale were going on in this way—the way not specified—Prince Peter would show him which had the most friends in the settlement. Some minutes later a second note came from Ragsdale, breathing wrath and consternation, but not more explicit than the first. Mr. Meyer put a bottle of claret in his pocket, hastened down the cliff, and came to the house of the prince. A crowd of men surrounded it, the friends referred to, or their van; it seems not known if they were armed, but their looks were martial. Prince Peter himself, although incensed, proved malleable in debate, owned it was disgraceful for the two best-educated men in Kalawao to quarrel, and consented to leave his friends behind and go alone with Mr. Meyer to the luna's. Ragsdale lived in a grass house on the foreland; it was garrisoned by some score of men with guns, axes, shovels, and fish spears. Ragsdale himself was on the watch, but the sight of two men coming empty-handed made him ashamed of his preparations and he received them civilly. A conversation followed; some misunderstandings were explained away; an apology handsomely offered by Ragsdale was handsomely accepted by the prince; the bottle of claret was drunk in company, and the friends on either side disbanded. Thus ended the alarm of war, and the opponents continued in a serviceable alliance until death divided them.

It was in the reign of Ragsdale that Father Damien arrived, May 1873. He draws no very favorable picture of the society that paid homage to King Billy; but the reign was efficient, and save for the episode of Prince Peter, quiet. So much could not be said for that of his critic and successor, Damien himself, whose term of office served only to publish the weakness of a noble man. He was rough in his ways and he had no control; authority was relaxed, the luna's life was threatened, and he was soon eager to resign. Two more conclude the list, Mr. Strahan, who was still alive at the time of my visit, and Mr. Ambrose Hutchinson, who still held the reins of office.

Mr. Strahan, born of Scottish parents in Philadelphia, ran away to sea in a whaler and deserted in Tahiti. He learned carpentering, coopering, and seamanship; sailed mate in ships, made copra in the Palmyras, worked on the guano islands, and led in all ways the career of the South Sea adventurer. For two years he lived in Easter Island, the isle of nameless gods and forgotten pieties. A mysterious sickness, brought from the mainland by labor slaves, struck and prostrated the population. Mr. Strahan was seen sometimes alone to go out fishing, and he made with his own hands a barrow to convey the corpses to the grave, and crutches on which the native clergyman might accompany the funerals. "That was my best time," said the old gentleman, regretfully. At last, when he was mate of a schooner, he chanced one day to be shaving, as I have received the story, in the cabin. "Good God, Strahan!" cried the captain, "you have cut off a piece of your ear." He had indeed, and did not know it; the plague, long latent in his blood, was now declared, and the wanderer found a home in Kalawao. As a luna he did well, reducing at once the previous discontents. He claims to have introduced coffee shops, sewing machines, musical instruments—"I wanted to put some life in the thing," says he—and the system of medals by which the drawing of double rations was at length prevented. Some of his claims are called in question; it is said he must certainly be under illusion as to the sewing machines and the musical instruments; but all agree as to the efficiency of his administration. His worst trouble arose by accident, and depicts well the jealous suspicion and the vain and passing agitations of a pauperized society. From a chance boat he purchased a load of native food which (as it had not been made expressly for the settlement) was packed in bundles larger than the regulation size. These he set his assistants to break up and weigh out afresh. Word of it got abroad; it was rumored that Strahan was secretly diminishing the rations; and he was suddenly surrounded as he rode by some fifty or a hundred horsemen menacing his life. "I sat right in my saddle like this. Says I: 'You may kill me; I'll be the sooner through with this leprosy. Why don't you do it?' I says: 'Barking dogs don't bite.' I was a hard old coon," added the ex-luna. In the progress of the disease, blindness at last unfitted him for further duty, and he now dwells in a cottage by the hospital, delighting to receive visitors, to recall his varied experiences, and to recite his poetry. "It's doggrel, that's what it is," he says. "I'm not an educated man, but the idea's there. You see," he adds, "I've got nothing to do but to sit here and think." The surroundings of his later life have lent a color to these musings, and he awaits death in his clean cottage, sightless: after so many joyous and so many rude adventures, so much plowing the sea, so much frequentation of fair islands, one subject inspires and occupies his verse; he will speak to you gladly of old comrades or old days of pleasure and peril; but when he takes his pen it is to treat, with womanly tenderness, of the child that is a leper.

One incident remains—that of the murder. The Kapiolani Home was founded in Oahu for clean children born within the precinct, and Mr. Meyer was instructed to obtain the consent of the parents. It was given (to their honor be it said) by all, and the condition made, that one of the parents should accompany each child upon a visit of inspection, was naturally granted. There was an old leper in the settlement, a widower, with a leper son and two clean daughters, children. He was himself too far advanced to be allowed beyond the precinct, and he asked and obtained leave for his son to accompany the children in his place. The steamer came late, about six at night, and the children and their friends were bundled on board with extreme, perhaps indecent, haste. The harbor master came breathing hurry, to a shed after the baggage, and found the old man sitting in despair upon his children's trunk. He bid him rise; was unanswered, possibly unheard; and roughly plucked the trunk from below the sitter. In a moment, and for the only time in the story of the

Lazaretto, savage instinct woke; a knife was drawn, the harbor master was slain, and before the pitiable homicide could be disarmed two more were wounded. Even justice feared to approach the settlement; the trial was held at a safe distance, on the island of Lanai, and the criminal sentenced to ten years in prison. Outside, the tale was used to infamous purpose, and, whether from political intrigue or in the wantonness of sentimentalism, magnified as a case of inhumanity to lepers.

The murder stands alone, as I have said, in the criminal annals of Kalawao. Brewing okolehao, or potato spirit, is the common offense, and occurs, or is discovered, about once in the two years; there have been besides a burglary or two, and occasional assaults, always about women. For even here, in the anteroom of the grave and among so marred a company, the ancient forces of humanity prevail. And from Ragsdale and Prince Peter, when the collision of their vanities embroiled the foreland, the partisans who gathered at their cry, filled with the ineradicable human readiness to shed blood upon a public difference; the horsemen who surrounded Strahan, calling for his life; Strahan himself, when he sat in the saddle and defied them; and the men who brawled, and the poor pair for whom they quarreled—all were lepers, maimed, defeatured, seated by an open grave. Yet upon this sheaf of anecdotes the influence of pauperism is plainly to be traced, while they might all be told, all understood, and leprosy not mentioned. Our normal forces, our whole limbs, even that expectation of days which we collate from actuarial tables—it seems there is nothing of which we may not be deprived, and still retain the gusto of existence. But perhaps mankind have scarce yet learned how mechanical, how involuntary, how fatal, or (if the reader pleases) how divine, is their immixture in the interests and the affairs of life.

Such is the story, such the Newgate calendar, of this scarce paralleled society, where all are lepers, stripped of their lands and families, prisoners without offense, sick unto death, already dead in law, and denied that chief regulator and moderator of men's lives, a daily task; where so many have besides been caught like bandits, lurking armed in woods, resisting to the blood, hauled in with violence; scarce sooner taken than tamed. They claimed to be outside the law; it seems they were men that did not want it, and without judges and police could do better than ourselves surrounded with protection and restraint.

✤ 8 ✤

THE LAZARETTO OF TODAY

The ideas of deformity and living decay have been burdensome to my imagination since the nightmares of childhood; and when I at last beheld, lying athwart the sunrise, the leper promontory and the bare town of Kalaupapa; when the first boat set forth laden with patients; when it was my turn to follow in the second, seated by two sisters on the way to their brave employment; when we drew near the landing stairs and saw them thronged with the dishonored images of God, horror and cowardice worked in the marrow of my bones.

The coming of the sisters had perhaps attracted an unusual attendance. To many of those who "meddle with cold iron" in the form of pens, any design of writing appears excuse sufficient for the most gross intrusion—perhaps, less fortunate, I have never attained to this philosophy—shame seized upon me to be there, among the many suffering and few helpers, useless and a spy; and I made my escape out of the throng and set forth on foot for Kalawao. It was still quite early morning, as I went with my bundles up the road. The air was cool, the level sunbeams struck overhead upon the pali, the birds were piping in the cliffside woods. I met many lepers riding hard, as though belated, toward the landing place; others sat in their doorways, and with those I exchanged salutations, with these I sometimes stopped and fell in talk. Some halfway over, Mr. Hutchinson met and mounted me; and I came at last to the guesthouse, and threw myself on the bed to sleep, tired indeed in mind and body, but at peace. It was not merely that the plunge was made, and I had steeled my heart against painful surroundings; but already, in the course of that morning walk, some of the worst of the painfulness had disappeared.

To the porch of a house in the outskirts of Kalaupapa I was summoned by a woman. She knew English, she was comely in face and person, of engaging manners, spoke with an affectionate gentleness, and regarded me with undissembled sympathy. In the course of our talk it leaked out she supposed me to be the new white leper, and when I had corrected the mistake a singular change appeared immediately in her face and manner. She had thought I was a leper, doomed, like herself, to spend my few last of days in that reclusion, and when she found that I was clean and free, and might look forward to the average life of man, her feeling was regret. In view of my own horrified thoughts of that disease and of the place I was then visiting, in view of the mountain outlaws, and of that scene on the beach of Hoʻokena so recently inscribed upon my memory, it was hard to understand her attitude. Yet I am persuaded such is (on the whole) the attitude of the Lazaretto. Horror, sorrow, all idea of resistance, all bitterness of regret have passed from the spirits of these sufferers, and the sick colony smiles upon its bed of death.

Nothing in the story of Molokai appears more culpable than that series of neglects by which the exiles were progressively pauperized: and, perhaps, nothing was more fortunate. Rations and no work are the attractions of the Lazaretto. Even he who has lain in the bush, and been long hunted, and perhaps taken at last in combat, savagely defending freedom, is soon emasculated in that pauper atmosphere; and the wildest settle down contented to their life as parasites. I heard two men discussing an escape. One was an official. "Ah," said he, referring to the fugitive, "he had not been long here!" And such I believe to be the fact, at least with natives; if they seek to escape at all, it is while they are new-caught. Yet more significant is the case of the clean *kokua*s. These, usually connections of the sick, allowed to accompany their wives, husbands, or children, are the working bees of the sad hive, the laborers, butchers, storekeepers, nurses, and gravediggers in that place of malady and folded hands. The surroundings, the few toilers looked upon by so many as delivered from all touch of need—the frequency of death, the brevity of prospect, the consequent estimation of the moment—might relax the fiber even of ardent and industrious races. In the Polynesian *kokua*s the result appears to be unmingled envy of a better state. They are peris at the gates of a paradise of rations. Dr. Swift had once in his hand a lancet charged with the virus of leprosy. "Come here," he cried, in a somewhat appalling pleasantry, to one of the *kokua*s, "come here and I will make a leper of you." The man advanced, rolling up his sleeve as he came. *Paris vaut bien une messe;* and, in the thought of this gentleman, rations are worth leprosy.

Within the precinct, to be leprous is the rule. The disease no longer awakens pity, nor do its deformities move shame in the patient or disgust in the beholder. Late one afternoon, as I rode from Kalaupapa, I saw in front of me, on a downward slope that leads to Kalawao, a group of natives returning from some junket. They wore their many-colored Sunday's best, bright wreaths of flowers hung (in the Hawaiian fashion) from their necks; the trade wind brought me strains of song and laughter; and I saw them gambol by the way, and the men and women chase and change places with each other as they came. They made from a distance an engaging picture; I had near forgotten in what distressful country my road lay, and I was amazed to see (as they approached) that out of that small company two were unhumanly defaced. The girl at Hoʻokena, a leper at large among the clean, held down her head. I was glad to find she would soon walk with face erect among her fellows, and perhaps be attended as a beauty. Yet more, she may even appear adorned and with applause upon a public stage; for plays and historical tableaux are among the chief diversions of the Lazaretto. And one thing is sure, the most disgraced of that unhappy crew may expect the consolations of love; love laughs at leprosy; and marriage is in use to the last stage of decay and the last gasp of life.

On the whole, the spectacle of life in this marred and moribund community, with its idleness, its furnished table, its horse riding, music, and gallantries, under the shadow of death, confounds the expectations of the visitor. He cannot observe with candor, but he must see it is not only good for the world but best for the lepers themselves to be thus set apart. The place is a huge hospital, but a hospital under extraordinary conditions, in which the disease, although both ugly and incurable, is of a slow advance; in which the patients are rarely in pain, often capable of violent exertion, all bent on pleasure, and all, within the limits of the precinct, free. From his abnormal state another norm arises, and not the patients only, but their doctors and helpers, half forget the habits of a healthy world. I have been present while the lay brother, Mr. Dutton, dressed the sores of his boy charges; he introduced them as they came with jesting comments on each case; and his pleasantries, which might have scattered a dinner party at home, were given and received with kindly smiles. "The hand of little emplorement hath the daintier sense." Chance had so arranged my life that I have been often constrained to visit infirmaries; in my case, the experience has been in vain; I have never crossed the doors of one without a contraction of the heart; and while I viewed the hospital at Kalawao, with Dr. Swift, or stood by as Mr. Dutton dressed his patients, I took in my breath like a groom. Nonetheless, and even as I winced, I felt that I was making, I must not say much of little, but more than needful of a great deal; admired and envied in vain the nonchalance of my guides; and recognized with gratitude that the lees of life, even in that place, were not without alleviation and resource.

The case of the children is by far the most sad; and yet, thanks to Damien and that great Hawaiian lady, the kind Mrs. Bishop, and to the kind sisters, their hardship has been minimized. Even the boys in the still rude boys' home at Kalawao appeared cheerful and youthful; they interchange diversions in the boys' way; are one week all for football, and the next the devotees of marbles or of kites; have fiddles, drums, guitars, and penny whistles; some can touch the organ, and all combine in concerts. As for the girls in the Bishop Home, of the many beautiful things I have been privileged to see in life, they, and what has been done for them, are not the least beautiful. When I came there first the sisters and the majority of the boarders were gone up the hill upon a weekly treat, guava hunting, and only Mother Mary Anne and the specially sick were left at home. I was told things which I heard with tears, of which I sometimes think at night, and which I spare the reader, I was shown the sufferers then at home; one, I remember, white with pain, the tears standing in her eyes. But, thank God, pain is not the rule in this revolting malady; and the general impression of the home was one of cheerfulness, cleanliness, and comfort. The dormitories were airy, the beds neatly made; at every bedhead was a trophy of Christmas cards, pictures, and photographs, some framed with shells, and all arranged with care and taste. In many of the beds, besides, a doll lay pillowed. I was told that, in that artificial life, the oldest and the youngest were equally concerned with these infantile playthings, and the dressmaking in particular was found an inexhaustible resource. Plays of their own arrangement were a favorite evening pastime. They had a croquet set, and it was my single useful employment, during my stay in the Lazaretto, to help them with that game.

I know not if the interest in croquet survived my departure, but it was lively while I stayed; and the last time I passed there, on my way to the steamer's boat and freedom, the children crowded to the fence and hailed and summoned me with cries of welcome. I wonder I found the heart to refuse the invitation.

I used to have an easy conscience when returning from these croquet parties. Should any reader desire to share the rare sensation, boy's toys, music, and musical instruments will be welcome at Kalawao, and such trifles as old Christmas cards and bright-colored remnants will serve to make beautiful the rooms, the dolls, and the maimed actresses of the Bishop Home. So much we may all do at a long range, and without risk or suffering. Nearer help is yet conceivable upon the part of some. And if a man be musical, cheerful, conversable, nothing of a rigorist, not burdened with a family, and smit with some incurable, perhaps some disfiguring complaint, it might cost him a few deep breaths at the beginning, but I know not where and how else he were so well employed as ministering to the brief gaiety of these afflicted.

9

THE FREE ISLAND

I wonder (I have just said) that I could refuse the invitation of these stricken children, but in truth, when the day came, my heart panted for deliverance. Before the *Mokoli'i* was yet announced I was already in the saddle, and the first boat carried me on board. It was near conveying me back again as well. Some flaw was in the wording of my pass, which allowed me specifically enough to enter the settlement, but said nothing of my leaving it; the steamer had been fined once before, and I was at first refused a passage. I had not known till then the eagerness of my impatience to be gone; it gave me persuasion; the captain relented, and it was not long before I was tossing at sea, eating untainted food, drinking clear sea air, and beholding the headland of the Lazaretto slip behind upon the starboard quarter.

The name of the whole large island of Molokai is sullied in the public mind, but Kalaupapa, Kalawao, and Waikolu, which make up the leper territory, form an inconsiderable fraction of its surface, and the rest is a free country of clean folk. Even the promontory itself has not yet been thirty years dedicated to sickness; its sad associations are still young, and in the legends of the race these melancholy scenes are peopled with warriors and fair dames. Just beyond Waikolu stood the fort of Ha'upu, of whose siege and fall readers may find the hyperbolical story in a recent volume; it was in these profound waters, where no ship may anchor, that the elastic Kana [a supernatural male being capable of "stretching" his body] waded unembarrassed, and the Lady Hina [goddess], from the battlements of her prison, looked across the sea of Kalawao.

Our first place of call on the free island was the cleft of Pelekunu. Dinner—which we ate upon the hatch, and which may have been good or bad, I know not, to me it was nectar and ambrosia—dinner was scarce over ere we were close under the cliffs, passed between them through a rent, and lay tossing in the jaws of a fiord full of spray and clamor. A few houses stood along the beach; the mountain soared behind, a mountain so impracticable that to cross the island takes a hard day's travel. The starboard surfboat was lowered, it pulled for the shore; right overhead, lads were running and leaping already on the ledges of the hill; the boat drew in; a man stood rocking in the bows; on the nearest vantage there stood over against him one of the lads of the shore; and these too, letter by letter, and watching the chances of the surf, exchanged the mails of Pelekunu. The scene rolled with the rolling of the ship; it passed amid so huge a clamor of the seas that as regards its human actors it might be said to pass in silence; it took but a breath or two of time, and it left (when we were forth again upon blue waters) no more than a roaring in my ears, and in the eyes of my mind a medley of tossing mountains, dancing boats, and bursting surges.

Beyond Pelekunu a vast face of mountain—three thousand feet, they said—plunges in the sea, from summit to base one unanimous, unbroken barrier to defy a cat, yet all green with contiguous forest, thick as a beast's fur, and growing, like fur, in swaths of divergent ply. This perpendicular bush in the time of the rains is all shot through with the silver of cascades. Even in the dry season, when I passed, the slot of them was like downward comb marks, and an attenuated gray mare's tail hung here and there, and dissipated as it fell. Island fellow passengers sought to point out to me a path about halfway up, by which men scramble, seeking the eggs of seabirds that nest populously in that hanging forest. I had never seen before, nor have I seen since, scenery so formidable as the island front of Molokai from Pelekunu to Wailau.

For Wailau we had a passenger, two pigs, and three sheep, besides the mails. Here a green valley runs back deep and tortuous among the mountains, the bed of a small stream; and about its mouth a single row of houses lines the beach, their windows flanking westward down the coast. Impassable surf broke at the very doorsteps; and far to seaward the sound of its dissolution hung already in our ears. Communication with the shore was beyond hope. We kept away again, bearing along with us the passenger, who had enjoyed the advantage to behold his destination from the deck, and had now before him a fair choice, either to land on the lee coast and laboriously pass the mountains, or to begin his voyage again in the coming week, to meet perhaps a second disappointment.

We came ashore about sundown at Pūko'o; a capital horse, which (had it been mine) I would not have lent to an apostle, was placed at my service; and the captain and I rode till it was black night along the leeward coast. It was cool, and threatened rain, and the twilight was soon obscured by overhanging clouds. We rode fast on a good highway, and saw indistinctly flitting by us a succession of canebrakes and taro patches, frequent churches—always in pairs, the Protestant and Catholic—and rare inhabited houses, piercing the darkness with their lights. About eight of the night, the sound of a mill advised us of our destination; we turned aside from the highway, and came to a house where a prodigious number of men with strong Irish speech sat in a dark veranda; within was a long table, where I was soon taking tea with a proportion of ladies; and in the middle region, in a pleasant parlor, grown girls and laughing children flourished as plenty (I thought) as mice. They were all of that class of Irish whom I cannot tell, save for a trifling variance of brogue, from my own folk of Scotland; persons of thoughtful, careful speech, observant subhumorously, and with those fine, plain manners which turn the laugh on class distinctions.

About half-past eight of the next day, the captain being long since gone to his ship, I took my leave of the McUrstens [McCorristons] in a fine rain which speedily cleared off. My guide was one Apaka, a stout, short, whiskered native, mounted on a white

punch that seemed to be his near connection. Maui
behind us towered into clouds and the shadow of
clouds. The bare opposite island of Lanai—the reef
far out, enclosing a dirty, shoal lagoon—a range of
fishponds, large as docks, and the slope of the sandy
beach on which we mostly rode, occupied the left
hand. On the right the mountain rose in steeps of red
clay and sprouts of disintegrated rock, sparsely dotted with the white-flowering cow thistle. Here and
there along the foreshore stood a lone pandanus, and
once a trinity of disheveled palms. In all the first part
of that journey, I recall but three houses and a single
church. Plenty of horses, kine, and sullen-looking
bulls were there; but not a human countenance.
"Where are the people?" I asked. *"Pau kanaka make.*
Done; people dead," replied Apaka, with the singular childish giggle which the traveler soon learns to
be a mark of Polynesian sensibility. "No people? No
houses?" I would cry, at the turn of every bay; and
back would come the antiphon: *"Pau kanaka make."*

We rode all the time by the side of the great fishponds, the labor (you would say) of generations. The
riches and the agriculture of Molokai awoke of yore
the envy of neighboring kings. Only last century upon
this island a battle was fought in which it has been
computed that thousands were engaged; and he who
made the computation, though he lived long after,
has seen and counted, when the wind blew aside the
sands, the multitude of bones and skulls. There remains the evidence of the churches, not yet old and
already standing in a desert, the monuments of vanished congregations. *Pau kanaka make.* A sense of
survival attended me upon my ride, and the nervous

laughter of Apaka sounded in my ears not quite un-pleasantly. The place of the dead is clean; there is a poetry in empty lands.

A greener track received us; smooth, shoreside grass was shaded with groves and islets of acacias; the hills behind, from the red color of the soil and the singularity of the formation, had the air of a bare Scottish moorland in the bleak end of autumn; and the resemblance set a higher value on the warmth of the sun and the brightness of the sea. I wakened sud-denly to remember Kalaupapa and my playmates of two days before. Could I have forgotten? was I happy again? had the shadow, the sorrow, and the obligation faded already?

The thought was still in my mind when the green track conducted us into Kaunakakai; a church among the acacias, a grove of coco palms, a pier in the la-goon, a few scattered houses, and a schoolhouse where we paused to gossip, the brown schoolboys observing us through the windows and exulting in the interrup-tion. Thence we must mount into that iron desert of the foothills, which we had skirted all the morning. Clouds of dust accompanied our march; rock and red clay, rock and red clay, cow thistles and cow thistles, and no other growing thing, surrounded us; all the while the sea and Lanai, and the desert western end of Molokai, spread wider and paler below us as we went. The horses, in the course of the ascent, began to snort and labor; the coat of the white punch was strangely altered into one of many hues, and his rider began to flail him with the bridle end. Next, we must descend into a narrow vale of rocks, where were candlenut trees and prickly pears in flower; it was deadly hot and dry in the valley, and Apaka's horse complained aloud. One more abrupt ascent, and we found we had climbed at last into the zone of rains and the sea wind. Downs spread about us clothed with grass and diversified with trees and cattle. The roots of the glens, which here (on the backbone of the isle) lie near together, were all thronged with candle-nuts shining like beeches in the spring; their slopes dotted with lehua, a small tree growing something like the cork, and bearing a red flower. Here and there were houses widely scattered, and chief among these the house of Mr. Meyer presides in a paradise of flowers and Monterey cypress, the doors standing open on trellised verandas, the sweet trade making a vital stir in all the chambers. Here he begins to grow old among his sons and fair daughters; and some two thousand feet below—a leap of half a minute—the lepers ride by the sea margin, and the boys of Kalawao play on their instruments and the girls of the Bishop Home arrange their bedside trophies.

For the whole slope of the isle and the channeling of watercourses run to the south; and to the north, a little beyond Meyer's door, the world abruptly stops. At the edge of the pali, the lehua trees are grown upon by a strong creeper, in whose embrace many stand dead; a yellowish moss like sheep's wool flutters from their boughs; they go over the edge, which is sheer and sudden like a battlement, in open order, leaning from the wind; and become immediately massed upon the face in thickets. The base cannot be seen; not many hundred feet below the wood comes to a profile, and stands relieved against the sea and the singular flat perspective of the promontory, blacker and bleaker to look down upon from this high station; the black cliffs bounding it, the white breakers creaming beyond, and beyond again the green belt of soundings shading swiftly into the profoundest blue of ocean. A strong sun threw out the details; Kalaupapa, the home, the churches, the houses drawn up in line like bathing machines, all distinct and bright like toys.

Here, where it began, only some two thousand feet higher, I bring to an end this visiting of Molokai. The whole length and breadth of the once busy isle I have either coasted by or ridden. And where are the people? where are the houses? where is the smoke of the fires? I see again Apaka riding by me on the leeward beach; I hear again the sound of his painful laughter and the words of his refrain: *"Pau kanaka make."*

10

ANOTHER MOLOKAI

. . . In 1890, when I was at Penrhyn [in the Tokelau group], Mr. Hird was supercargo on the *Janet
Nicoll*; and knowing I had visited the Lazaretto on
Molokai, he called me in consultation. "It is strange,"
said he. "When I was here there was no such thing
as leprosy upon the island; and now there seems a
great deal. Look at that man, and tell me what you
think." The man was leprous as Naaman.

The story goes that a leper escaped from Molokai
in an open boat and landed, some say in Penrhyn,
some say first in Manihiki. There are many authentic
boat voyages difficult to credit; but this of thirty
degrees due north and south, and from the one trade
to the other across the equatorial doldrums, ranks
with the most extraordinary. We may suppose the
westerly current to have been entirely intermitted,
the easterly strong, and the fugitive well supplied
with food. Or we may explain the tale to be a legend,
framed to conceal the complaisance of some ill-judg-
ing skipper. One thing at least is sure: a Hawaiian

leper, in an advanced stage of the disease, and admitting that he had escaped from Molokai, appeared suddenly in these distant islands, and was seen by Mr. H. J. Moors of Apia walking at large in Penrhyn. Mr. Moors is not quite certain of the date, for he visited the atoll in 1883 and again in 1884; but another of my neighbors, Mr. Harper, was trading in Penrhyn all the first year. He saw nothing of the Hawaiian, and this pins us to the later date. I am tediously particular on this point, because the result is amazing. Seven years is supposed to be the period of leprous incubation; and the whole of my tale, from the first introduction of the taint to the outbreak of a panic on the island, passes (at the outside) in a little more than six. At the time when we should have scarce looked for the appearance of the earliest case, the population was already steeped in leprosy.

The Polynesians assuredly derive from Asia; and Asia, since the dawn of history, has been a camping ground for this disease. Of two things, either the Polynesian left, ere the disease began, and is now for the first time exposed to the contagion, or he has been so long sequestered that Asiatic leprosy has had the time to vary, and finds in him a virgin soil. The facts are not clear; we are told, on one hand, that some indigenous form of the disease was known in Samoa within the memory of man; we are assured, on the other, that there is not a name for it in any island language. There is no doubt, at least, about the savage rapidity with which it spreads when introduced. And there is none that, when a leper is first seen, the islanders approach him without disaffection and are never backward to supply him with a wife. I find this singular; for few races are more sensitive to beauty, of which their own affords so high a standard; and I have observed that when the symptoms are described to him in words, the islander displays a high degree of horror and disgust. His stringent ideals of courtesy and hospitality and a certain debile kindliness of disposition must explain his conduct. As for the marriage, the stranger once received, it follows as a thing of course. To refuse the male is still considered in most parts of Polynesia a rather unlovely rigor in the female; and if a man be disfigured, I believe it would be held a sort of charity to console his solitude. A kind island girl might thus go to a leper's bed in something of the same spirit as we visit the sick at home with tracts and pounds of tea.

The waif who landed on Penrhyn was much marred with the disease; his head deformed with growths; a thing for children to flee from screaming. Yet he was received with welcome, entertained in families, and a girl was found to be his wife. It is hard to be just to this Hawaiian. Doubtless he was a man of a wild strain of blood, a lover of liberty and life; doubtless he had harbored in the high woods and the rains, a spectral Robin Hood, armed to defend his wretched freedom; perhaps he was captured fighting; and of one thing we may be sure, that he had escaped early from the Lazaretto, still untamed, still hot with resentment. His boat voyage was a discipline well fitted to inspire grave thoughts; in him it may have only sharpened the desire of pleasure; for to certain shallow natures the imminence of death is but a whet. In his own eyes he was an innocent prisoner escaped, the victim of a nameless and senseless tyranny. What did he ask? To taste the common lot of men, to sit with the house folk, to hear the evensong, to share in the day's gossip, to have a wife like others, and to see children round his knees. He landed in Penrhyn, enjoyed for a while simple pleasures, died, and bequeathed to his entertainers a legacy of doom.

They were early warned. Mr. Moors warned them in 1884, and they made light of his predictions, the long incubation of the malady deceiving them. The leper lived among them; no harm was seen. He died, and still there was no harm. It would be interesting, it is probably impossible, to learn how soon the plague appeared. By the midst of 1890, at least, the island was dotted with lepers, and the *Janet Nicoll* had not long gone before the islanders awoke to an apprehension of their peril. I have mentioned already traits which they share with their Paumotuan kindred; their conduct in this hour of awakening is another. There were certain families—twenty, I was told; we may imply a corrective and guess ten—entirely contaminated; the clean waited on these sick and bade them leave the settlement. Some six years before they had opened their doors to a stranger; now they must close them on their next of kin.

It chanced that among the tainted families were some of chief importance, some that owned the land of the village. It was their first impulse to resent the measure of expulsion.

"The land is ours," they argued. "If any are to leave, let it be you," and they were thought to have answered well; "let them stay" was the reconsidered verdict; and the clean people began instead to prepare their own secession. The coming of the missionary ship decided otherwise; the lepers were persuaded; a *motu* [islet] of some size, hard by the south entrance, was now named Molokai, after its sad original; and thither, leaving their lands and the familiar village, self-doomed, self-sacrificed, the infected families went forth into perpetual exile.

The palms of their lost village are easily in view from Molokai. The sequestered may behold the smoke rise from their old home; they can see the company of boats skim forth with daylight to the place of diving. And they have yet nearer sights. A pier has been built in the lagoon; a boat comes at intervals, leaves food upon its seaward end, and goes again, the lepers not entering on the pier until it be gone. Those on the beach, those in the boat, old friends and kinsfolk thus behold each other for a moment silently. The girl who bid Mr. Hird flee from the settlement opened her heart to him on his last visit. She would never again set eyes, she told him, on her loved ones, and when he reminded her that she might go with the boat and see them from a distance on the beach, "Never!" she cried. If she went, if she saw them, her heart would pluck her from the boat; she must leap on the pier, she must run to the beach, she must speak again with the lost; and with the act the doors of the prison isle would close upon herself. So sternly is the question of leprosy now viewed, under a native rule, in Penrhyn.

Long may it so continue! and I would I could infect with a like severity every isle of the Pacific. But self-indulgence and sentiment menace instead the mere existence of the island race; perhaps threaten our own with a new struggle against an enemy refreshed. Nothing is less proved than this peril to ourselves; yet it is possible. To our own syphilis we are inured, but the syphilis of eastern Asia slays us; and a new variety of leprosy, cultivated in the virgin soil of Polynesian races, might prove more fatal than we dream.

So that ourselves, it may be, are no strangers to the case; it may be it was for us the men of Penrhyn resigned their acres, and when the defaced chimera sailed from Molokai, bringing sorrow and death to isles of singing, we also, and our babes may have been the target of his invisible arrows. But it needs not this. The thought of that hobgoblin boatman alone upon the sea, of the perils he escaped, of the evil he lavished on the world, may well strike terror in the minds even of the distant and the unconcerned. In mine, at the memory of my termagant minstrel, hatred glows.

II

LETTERS FROM HAWAII

LETTERS FROM HAWAII

The unabridged letters written by Stevenson and his wife from Hawaii are more revealing of their immediate personal feelings than are the polished chapters of "The Eight Islands." Unless otherwise noted, the source is The Letters of Robert Louis Stevenson, *edited by Sidney Colvin, 4 vols., New York: Charles Scribner's Sons, 1911. The items have been numbered for convenience in reference.*

1. To E. L. Burlingame

Edward Livermore Burlingame (1848–1922) was editor of Scribner's Magazine *from 1887 to 1914.*

Honolulu, January 1889

MY DEAR BURLINGAME,

Here at last I have arrived. We could not get away from Tahiti till Christmas Day, and then had thirty days of calms and squalls, a deplorable passage. This has thrown me all out of gear in every way. I plunge into business.

1. *The Master.* Herewith go three more parts. You see he grows in bulk; this making ten already, and I am not sure yet if I can finish it in an eleventh; which shall go to you *quam primum*—I hope by next mail.

2. *Illustrations to M.* I totally forgot to try to write to Hole. It was just as well, for I find it impossible to forecast with sufficient precision. You had better throw off all this and let him have it at once. *Please do: all, and at once: see further;* and I should hope he would still be in time for the later numbers. The three pictures I have received are so truly good that I should bitterly regret having the volume imperfectly equipped. They are the best illustrations I have seen since I don't know when.

3. *Money.* Tomorrow the mail comes in, and I

hope it will bring me money either from you or home, but I will add a word on that point.

4. My address will be Honolulu—no longer yacht *Casco,* which I am packing off—till probably April.

5. As soon as I am through with *The Master,* I shall finish *The Game of Bluff*—now rechristened *The Wrong Box.* This I wish to sell, cash down. It is of course copyright in the States; and I offer it to you for five thousand dollars. Please reply on this by return. Also please tell the typewriter who was so good as to be amused by our follies that I am filled with admiration for his piece of work.

6. *Master* again. Please see that I haven't the name of the governor of New York wrong (1764 is the date) in part ten. I have no book of reference to put me right. Observe you now have up to August inclusive in hand, so you should begin to feel happy.

Is this all? I wonder, and fear not. Henry the Trader has not yet turned up: I hope he may tomorrow, when we expect a mail. Not one word of business have I received either from the States or England, nor anything in the shape of coin; which leaves me in a fine uncertainty and quite penniless on these islands. H.M. [King Kalākaua] (who is a gentleman of a courtly order and much tinctured with letters) is very polite; I may possibly ask for the position of palace doorkeeper. My voyage has been a singular mixture of good and ill fortune. As far as regards interest and material, the fortune has been admirable; as far as regards time, money, and impediments of all kinds, from squalls and calms to rotten masts and sprung spars, simply detestable. I hope you will be interested to hear of two volumes on the wing. The cruise itself, you are to know, will make a big volume with appendices; some of it will first appear as (what they call) letters in some of M'Clure's papers. I believe the book when ready will have a fair measure of serious interest: I have had great fortune in finding old songs and ballads and stories, for instance, and have many singular instances of life in the last few years among these islands.

The second volume is of ballads. You know "Ticonderoga." I have written another: "The Feast of Famine," a Marquesan story. A third is half done: "The Song of Rahero," a genuine Tahitian legend. A fourth dances before me. A Hawaiian fellow this, "The Priest's Drought," or some such name. If, as I half suspect, I get enough subjects out of the islands, "Ticonderoga" shall be suppressed, and we'll call the volume *South Sea Ballads*. In health, spirits, renewed interest in life, and, I do believe, refreshed capacity for work, the cruise has proved a wise folly. Still we're not home, and (although the friend of a crowned head) are penniless upon these (as one of my correspondents used to call them) "lovely but *fatil* islands." By the way, who wrote the *Lion of the Nile*? My dear sir, that is Something Like. Overdone in bits, it has a true thought and a true ring of language. Beg the anonymous from me, to delete (when he shall republish) the two last verses, and end on 'the lion of the Nile.' One Lampman has a good sonnet on a "Winter Evening" in, I think, the same number: he seems ill named, but I am tempted to hope a man is not always answerable for his name. For instance, you would think you knew mine. No such matter. It is—at your service and Mr. Scribner's and that of all of the faithful—Teriitera (pray pronounce Tayree-Tayra) or (*gallicé*) Téri-téra.

R.L.S.

More when the mail shall come.

I am an idiot. I want to be clear on one point. Some of Hole's drawings must of course be too late; and yet they seem to me so excellent I would fain have the lot complete. It is one thing for you to pay for drawings which are to appear in that soul-swallowing machine, your magazine: quite another if they are only to illustrate a volume. I wish you to take a brisk (even a fiery) decision on the point; and let Hole know. To resume my desultory song, I desire you would carry the same fire (hereinbefore suggested) into your decision on *The Wrong Box*; for in my present state of benighted ignorance as to my affairs for the last seven months—I know not even whether my house or my mother's house have been let—I desire to see something definite in front of me—outside the lot of palace doorkeeper. I believe the said *Wrong Box* is a real lark; in which, of course, I may be grievously deceived; but the typewriter is with me. I may also be deceived as to the numbers of *The Master* now going and already gone; but to me they seem First Chop, sir, First Chop. I hope I shall pull off that damned ending; but it still depresses me: this is your doing, Mr. Burlingame: you would have it there and then, and I fear it—I fear that ending.

R.L.S.

LETTERS FROM HAWAII

2. To Charles Baxter

Baxter, almost two years older than Stevenson, was his close friend throughout life; they met at the University of Edinburgh, and for years, even after Stevenson's death, Baxter was his business and literary agent in Britain. R.L.S. was more frank with Baxter than with any other of his many correspondents.

Honolulu, February 8th, 1889

MY DEAR CHARLES,

Here we are at Honolulu, and have dismissed the yacht and lie here till April anyway in a fine state of haze, which I am yet in hopes some letter of yours (still on the way) may dissipate. No money, and not one word as to money! However, I have got the yacht paid off in triumph, I think; and though we stay here impignorate, it should not be for long, even if you bring us no extra help from home. The cruise has been a great success, both as to matter, fun, and health; and yet, Lord, man! we're pleased to be ashore! Yon was a very fine voyage from Tahiti up here, but—the dry land's a fine place too, and we don't mind squalls any longer, and eh, man, that's a great thing. Blow, blow, thou wintry wind, thou hast done me no appreciable harm beyond a few gray hairs! Altogether, this foolhardy venture is achieved, and if I have but nine months of life and any kind of health, I shall have both eaten my cake and got it back again with usury. But man, there have been days when I felt guilty, and thought I was in no position for the head of a house.

93

Your letter and accounts is doubtless at S.F. and will reach me in course. My wife is no great shakes: she is the one who has suffered most. My mother has had a Huge Old Time. Lloyd is first chop. I so well that I do not know myself—sea bathing, if you please, and what is far more dangerous, entertaining and being entertained by his Majesty [Kalākaua] here, who is a very fine, intelligent fellow, but O, Charles! what a crop for the drink! He carries it, too, like a mountain with a sparrow on its shoulders. We calculated five bottles of champagne in three hours and a half (afternoon) and the sovereign quite presentable, although perceptibly more dignified, at the end.

Valentin [Roch, the maid] leaves us here, to mutual glee. Stop her private wages, and be ready (when she applies) to give her her little stock. It has been the usual tale of the maid on board the yacht.—This reminds me, I believe I poured forth my sorrows over my captain in your ear. Patience and time have quite healed these conflicts; we do what we want now, and the captain is a trusted friend. It *did* require patience in the beginning, but the seed has borne a most plentiful crop, and we feel quite proud of our tame captain, and (as I say) really like the man.

I have very little time by this mail, so hurry all I can. I was overjoyed at the news of the Henley baby; it should go far to heal that household. I have no word from him, and shall not try to write in the midst of my scurry. He little understands the harm he did me; but I am sure, upon all our cruise, the number of times we—all of us—longed for his presence would show it was no change of liking for him that we feel.

For all that, time has not diminished my fear of him, and I doubt if I ever desire to correspond again. As for Katharine, I had an answer to my appeal, which settled that matter; I do not wish to see her. All these clouds, and the extraordinary health I enjoy and variety of interests I find among these islands, would tempt me to remain here—only for Lloyd, who is not well placed in such countries for a permanency, and a little for Colvin, to whom I feel I owe a sort of filial duty. And these two considerations will no doubt bring me back—to go to bed again—in England. I will write again soon, and beg for all news of the Henleys and all friends and beloved enemies.

Yours ever affectionately,
R.L.S.

3. To R. A. M. Stevenson

"Cousin Bob"—Robert Alan Mowbray Stevenson, son of the author's Uncle Alan and three years older than R.L.S.—went to Cambridge and later was a painter in France. In 1889 he was professor of fine art at the University of Liverpool.

Honolulu, February 1889

MY DEAR BOB,

My extremely foolhardy venture is practically over. How foolhardy it was I don't think I realized. We had a very small schooner, and, like most yachts, overrigged and oversparred, and like many American yachts, on a very dangerous sail plan. The waters we sailed in are, of course, entirely unlighted, and very badly charted; in the Dangerous Archipelago, through which we were fools enough to go, we were perfectly in ignorance of where we were for a whole night and half the next day, and this in the midst of invisible islands and rapid and variable currents; and we were lucky when we found our whereabouts at last. We have twice had all we wanted in the way of squalls; once, as I came on deck, I found the green sea over the cockpit coamings and running down the companion like a brook to meet me; at that same moment the foresail sheet jammed and the captain had no knife; this was the only occasion on the cruise that ever I set a hand to a rope, but I worked like a Trojan, judging the possibility of hemorrhage better than the certainty of drowning. Another time I saw a rather singular thing: our whole ship's company as pale as paper from the captain to the cook; we had a black squall astern on the port side and a white squall ahead to starboard; the complication passed off innocuous, the black squall only fetching us with its tail, and the white one slewing off somewhere else. Twice we were a long while (days) in the close vicinity of hurricane weather, but again luck prevailed, and we saw none of it. These are dangers incident to these seas and small craft. What was an amazement, and at the same time a powerful stroke of luck, both our masts were rotten, and we found it out—I was going to say in time, but it was stranger and luckier than that. The head of the mainmast hung over so that hands were afraid to go to the helm; and less than three weeks before—I am not sure it was more than a fortnight—we had been nearly twelve hours beating off the lee shore of Eimeo (or Moorea, next island to Tahiti) in half a gale of wind with a violent head sea: she would neither tack nor wear once, and had to be boxed off with the mainsail—you can imagine what an ungodly show of kites we carried—and yet the mast stood. The very day after that, in the southern bight of Tahiti, we had a near squeak, the wind suddenly coming calm; the reefs were close in with, my eye! what a surf! The pilot thought we were gone, and the captain had a boat cleared, when a lucky squall came to our rescue. My wife, hearing the order given about the boats, remarked to my mother, "Isn't that nice? We shall soon be ashore!" Thus does the female mind unconsciously skirt along the verge of eternity. Our voyage up here was most disastrous—calms, squalls, head sea, waterspouts of rain, hurricane weather all about, and we in the midst of the hurricane season, when even the hopeful builder and owner of the yacht had pronounced these seas unfit for her. We ran out of food, and were quite given up for lost in Honolulu: people had ceased to speak to Belle [Isobel Osbourne Strong] about the *Casco,* as a deadly subject.

But the perils of the deep were part of the program; and though I am very glad to be done with them for a while and comfortably ashore, where a squall does not matter a snuff to anyone, I feel pretty sure I shall want to go to sea again ere long. The dreadful risk I took was financial, and double-headed. First, I had to sink a lot of money in the cruise, and if I didn't get health, how was I to get it back? I have got health to a wonderful extent; and as I have the most interesting matter for my book, bar accidents, I ought to get all I have laid out and a profit. But, second (what I own I never considered till too late), there was the danger of collisions, of damages and heavy repairs, of disablement, towing, and salvage; indeed, the cruise might have turned round and cost me double. Nor will this danger be quite over till I hear the yacht is in San Francisco; for though I have shaken the dust of her deck from my feet, I fear (as a point of law) she is still mine till she gets there.

From my point of view, up to now the cruise has been a wonderful success. I never knew the world was so amusing. On the last voyage we had grown so used to sea life that no one wearied, though it lasted a full month, except Fanny, who is always ill. All the time our visits to the islands have been more like dreams than realities: the people, the life, the beachcombers, the old stories and songs I have picked up, so interesting; the climate, the scenery, and (in some places) the women, so beautiful. The women are handsomest in Tahiti, the men in the Marquesas; both as fine types as can be imagined. Lloyd reminds me, I have not told you one characteristic incident of the cruise from a semi-naval point of view. One night we were going ashore in Anaho Bay; the most awful noise on deck; the breakers distinctly audible in the cabin; and there I had to sit below, entertaining in my best style a negroid native chieftain, much the worse for rum! You can imagine the evening's pleasure.

This naval report on cruising in the South Seas would be incomplete without one other trait. On our voyage up here I came one day into the dining room, the hatch in the floor was open, the ship's boy was below with a baler, and two of the hands were carrying buckets as for a fire; this meant that the pumps had ceased working.

One stirring day was that in which we sighted Hawaii. It blew fair, but very strong; we carried jib, foresail, and mainsail, all single-reefed, and she carried her lee rail under water and flew. The swell the heaviest I have ever been out in—I tried in vain to estimate the height, *at least* fifteen feet—came tearing after us about a point and a half off the wind. We had the best hand—old Louis—at the wheel; and, really, he did nobly, and had noble luck, for it never caught us once. At times it seemed we must have it; old Louis would look over his shoulder with the queerest look and dive down his neck into his shoulders; and then it missed us somehow, and only sprays came over our quarter, turning the little outside lane of deck into a mill race as deep as to the cockpit coamings. I never remember anything more delightful and exciting. Pretty soon after we were lying absolutely becalmed under the lee of Hawaii, of which we had been warned; and the captain never confessed he had done it on purpose, but when accused, he smiled. Really, I suppose he did quite right, for we stood committed to a dangerous race, and to bring her to the wind would have been rather a heart-sickening maneuver.

R.L.S.

4. To Marcel Schwob

Among the accumulated letters awaiting Stevenson at Honolulu were two from the distinguished French scholar

TRAVELS IN HAWAII

Marcel Schwob (1867–1905). In them Schwob, a novelist and translator, paid homage to the Scottish author, and was briefly but warmly thanked. Late in 1890, Schwob was to ask Stevenson's permission to translate some of his works into French.

Honolulu, Sandwich Islands, February 8th, 1889

DEAR SIR,

I thank you—from the midst of such a flurry as you can imagine, with seven months' accumulated correspondence on my table—for your two friendly and clever letters. Pray write me again. I shall be home in May or June, and not improbably shall come to Paris in the summer. Then we can talk; or in the interval I may be able to write, which is today out of the question. Pray take a word from a man of crushing occupations, and count it as a volume. Your little *conte* is delightful. Ah yes, you are right, I love the eighteenth century; and so do you, and have not listened to its voice in vain.—The Hunted One,

ROBERT LOUIS STEVENSON

5. TO CHARLES BAXTER

Honolulu, March 8th, 1889

MY DEAR CHARLES,

At last I have the accounts: the doer has done excellently, and in the words of Galpin, "I reciprocate every step of your behavior." Only upon one point would I protest, in re my mother. (1) The house is hers; she might live in it if she chose and pay no rent to the trust; therefore, if she lets it, the rent is hers, and (in my contention) the trust has nothing to do with it. But (2) suppose you have some argument I do not follow which disposes of No. 1, I cannot see how you are to charge her with the rent received for the use of the house during the winter *before* my father's death. It was let then to meet extra expenses in the South; the extra expenses were incurred by my father; why, then, is my mother to be charged with the covering sum? I see no answer to that, anyway. And still, if I am dull and there should be a reason, I should like to make up my mother's money to what it was. Possibly we had better wait to decide this till we meet, so that I can make sure I follow.—The £5 and £20 paid on account of my mother is all right: let it slide. I used to embezzle from her: turn about is fair play.

Quite right you were, of course, about Bob, Henley, and the book of verses. Let Bob's interest slide: it's only an annoyance to him and bookkeeping for your clerks; to me it would not make the change of a hair. I send a letter for Bob in your care, as I don't know his Liverpool address, by which (for he is to show you part of it) you will see we have got out of this adventure—or hope to have—with wonderful fortune. I have the retrospective horrors on me when I think of the liabilities I incurred, but thank God I think I'm in port again, and I have found one climate in which I can enjoy life. Even Honolulu is too cold for me, but the South Isles were a heaven upon earth to a poor catarrhal party like Johns'one. We think, as Tahiti is too complete a banishment, to try Madeira. It's only a week from England, good communications, and I suspect in climate and scenery not unlike my own dear islands; in people, alas, there can be no comparison. But friends could go, and I could come in summer; so I should not be quite cut off.

Lloyd and I have finished a story, *The Wrong Box*. If it is not funny, I'm sure I don't know what is. I have split over writing it. Since I have been here, I have been toiling like a galley slave: three numbers of *The Master* to rewrite; five chapters of *The Wrong Box* to write and rewrite; and about five hundred lines of a narrative poem ["The Feast of Famine"] to write, rewrite, and re-rewrite. Now I have *The Master* waiting me for its continuation—two numbers more; when that's done, I shall breathe.

This spasm of activity has been chequered with champagne parties. Happy and Glorious *Hawai'i pono'ī nānā i kou mō'ī* (Native Hawaiians, dote upon your monarch!)—Hawaiian "God Save the King." (In addition to my other labors I am learning the language with a native munshi.) Kalākaua is a terrible companion: a bottle of fizz is like a glass of sherry to him; he thinks nothing of five or six in an afternoon as a whet for dinner. Look here: Van Laun, Edmonstone, Charles Mackay, and Sam Bough [various acquaintances]—he could have taken all four, one up, another down; as for you, you poor creature, he could settle you before breakfast. You should see a photograph of our party after an afternoon with H.H.M. [His Hawaiian Majesty]: my! what a crew! The proud drunkenness of Lloyd, the soppy swan-neckery of R.L.S., my mother—let us draw a veil till you see it. Yours ever affectionately,

ROBERT LOUIS STEVENSON

I enclose one of many income tax things I have received. What's wrong?

My dear friend, This is only to show that my heart is in the right place, though my body is not. It, alas, should [be] in Tautira with my well-beloved "savages," as they are fond of calling themselves. I am really better than I have been for some time. I *believe* the thing in my throat is gone, though I am nervous about it, and imagine that it is coming back when it is not. Louis is wonderful, and Lloyd is quite the literary man. It was very saddening to hear of poor Mrs. Henley's death, and most unexpected. I hope she passed away with as much comfort as one may. She had not too much in life. I had meant to write to Anna, congratulating her on the new acquisition, but somehow I can't write letters. My love to you all.

F. V DE G. S.

6. To SIDNEY COLVIN

Sidney Colvin (1845–1927) was a literary and art critic who as early as 1873 encouraged the youthful R.L.S. to write. He served as Slade Professor of Fine Art at Cambridge (1873–1885) and keeper of prints and drawings at the British Museum (1884–1912). He was knighted in 1921. As an intimate friend of Stevenson, Colvin edited the four-volume collection of the author's letters, as well as Vailima Letters *(1895), written to him from Samoa, and the Edinburgh edition of the collected works (1894–1898). "Ill health and pressing preoccupations" had kept Colvin from writing to Stevenson during the previous autumn and winter, along with uncertainty whether his letters would be delivered.*

TRAVELS IN HAWAII

Honolulu, March 1889

MY DEAR COLVIN,

Still not a word from you! I am utterly cast down;
but I will try to return good for evil and for once
give you news. We are here in the suburb of Honolulu in a rambling house or set of houses in a great
garden.

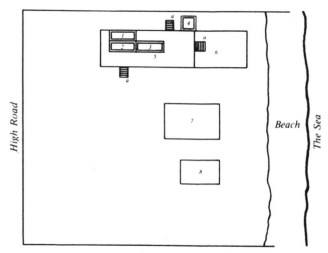

a a a, stairs up to balcony.

1. Lloyd's room. 2. My mother's room. 3. A room
kept dark for photographs. 4. The kitchen. 5. Balcony. 6. The lanai, an open room or summer parlor,
partly surrounded with Venetian shutters, in part
quite open, which is the living room. 7. A crazy, dirty
cottage used for the arts. 8. Another crazy, dirty
cottage, where Fanny and I live. The town is some
three miles away, but the house is connected by telephone with the chief shops, and the tramway runs
to within a quarter of a mile of us. I find Honolulu

a beastly climate after Tahiti and have been in bed a little; but my colds *took on no catarrhal symptom,* which is staggeringly delightful. I am studying Hawaiian with a native, a Mr. Joseph Poepoe, a clever fellow too: the tongue is a little bewildering; I am reading a pretty story in native—no, really it is pretty, although wandering and wordy; highly pretty with its continual traffic from one isle to another of the soothsayer, pursuing rainbows. Fanny is, I think, a good deal better on the whole, having profited like me by the tropics; my mother and Lloyd are first-rate. I do not think I have heard from you since last May; certainly not since June; and this really frightens me. Do write, even now. Scribner's Sons it should be; we shall probably be out of this some time in April, home some time in June. But the world whirls to me perceptibly, a mass of times and seasons and places and engagements, and seas to cross, and continents to traverse, so that I scarce know where I am. Well, I have had a brave time. *Et ego in Arcadia*— though I don't believe Arcadia was a spot upon Tahiti. I have written another long narrative poem: the "Song of Rahero." Privately, I think it good: but your ominous silence over the "Feast of Famine" leads me to fear we shall not be agreed. Is it possible I have wounded you in some way? I scarce like to dream that it is possible; and yet I know too well it may be so. If so, don't write, and you can pitch into me when we meet. I am, admittedly, as mild as London Stout now; and the Old Man Virulent much a creature of the past. My dear Colvin, I owe you and Fleeming Jenkin, the two older men who took the trouble, and knew how to make a friend of me, everything that I have or am: if I have behaved ill, just hold on and give me a chance, you shall have the slanging of me and I bet I shall prefer it to this silence.—Ever, my dear Colvin, your most affectionate

R.L.S.

7. From Mrs. R. L. Stevenson to Mrs. Sitwell

A charming friend ever since Stevenson met her first in 1873 was Mrs. Albert Sitwell, who had separated from her clergyman husband about that time. Almost twelve years the author's senior, "Fanny"—born Frances Jane Fetherstonhaugh—was a talented bluestocking who also became a friend of Stevenson's wife. At the age of sixty-two, in 1901, Mrs. Sitwell was to marry Sidney Colvin, Stevenson's editor. The letter below was the first to apprise friends in England that the Stevensons would prolong their voyage among the Pacific islands.

Honolulu, toward the end of March 1889

MY DEAR FRIEND,

Louis has improved so wonderfully in the delicious islands of the South Seas that we think of trying yet one more voyage. We are a little uncertain as to how we shall go, whether in a missionary ship, or by hiring schooners from point to point, but the "unregenerate" islands we must see. I suppose we shall be off sometime in June, which will fetch us back to England in another year's time. You could hardly believe it if you could see Louis now. He looks as well as he ever did in his life, and has had no sign of cough or hemorrhage (begging pardon of Nemesis) for many months. It seems a pity to return to England until his health is firmly reestablished, and also a pity not to see all that we can see quite easily starting from this place: and which will be our only opportunity in life. Of course there is the usual risk from hostile natives, and the horrible sea, but a positive risk is so much more wholesome than a negative one, and it is all such joy to Louis and Lloyd. As for me, I hate the sea, and am afraid of it (though no one will believe that because in time of danger I do not make an outcry—nevertheless I *am* afraid of it, and it is not kind to me), but I love the tropic weather, and the wild people, and to see my two boys so happy. Mrs. Stevenson is going back to Scotland in May, as she does not like to be longer away from her old sister, who has been very ill. And besides, we do not feel justified in taking her to the sort of places we intend to visit. As for me, I can get comfort out of very rough surroundings for my people, I can work hard and enjoy it; I can even shoot pretty well, and though I "don't want to fight, by jingo if I must," why I can. I don't suppose there will be any occasion for that sort of thing—only in case.

I am not quite sure of the names, but I *think* our new cruise includes the Gilberts, the Fijis, and the Solomons. A letter might go from the Fijis; Louis will write the particulars, of which I am not sure. As for myself, I have had more cares than I was really fit for. To keep house on a yacht is no easy thing. When Louis and I broke loose from the ship and lived alone amongst the natives I got on very well. It was when I was deathly seasick, and the question was put to me by the cook, "What shall we have for the cabin dinner, what for tomorrow's breakfast, what for lunch? and what about the sailors' food? Please come and look at the biscuits, for the weevils have got into them, and show me how to make yeast that will rise of itself, and smell the pork which seems pretty high, and give me directions about making a pudding with molasses—and what is to be done about the bugs?"—etc., etc. In the midst of heavy dangerous weather, when I was lying on the floor clutching a basin, down comes the mate with a cracked head, and I must needs cut off the hair matted with blood, wash and dress the wound, and administer restoratives. I do not like being "the lady of the yacht," but ashore! O, then I felt I was repaid for all. I wonder did any of my letters from beautiful Tautira ever come to hand, with the descriptions of our life with Louis' adopted brother Ori a Ori? Ori wrote to us, if no one else did, and I mean to give you a translation of his letter. It begins with our native names.

Tautira, Dec. 26th, 1888

To Teriitera (Louis) and Tapina Tutu (myself) and Aromaiterai (Lloyd) and Teiriha (Mrs. Stevenson) salutation in the true Jesus.

I make you to know my great affection. At the hour when you left us, I was filled with tears; my wife, Rui Tehini, also, and all of my household. When you embarked I felt a great sorrow. It is for this that I went upon the road, and you looked from that ship, and I looked at you on the ship with great grief until you had raised the anchor and hoisted the sails. When the ship started, I ran along the beach to see you still; and when you were on the open sea I cried out to you, "farewell, Louis": and when I was coming back to my house I seemed to hear your voice crying "Rui, farewell." Afterwards I watched the ship as long as I could until the night fell; and when it was dark I said to myself, "If I had wings I should fly to the ship to meet you, and to sleep amongst you, so that I might be able to come back to shore and to tell Rui Tehini, 'I have slept upon the ship of Teriitera.'" After that we passed that night in the impatience of grief. Towards eight o'clock I seemed to hear your voice, "Teriitera— Rui—here is the hour for putter and tiro" (cheese and syrup). I did not sleep that night, thinking continually of you, my very dear friend, until the morning: being then awake I went to see Tapina Tutu on her bed, and alas, she was not there. Afterwards I looked into your rooms; they did not please me as they used to do. I did not hear your voice crying, "Hail, Rui." I thought then that you had gone, and that you had left me. Rising up I went to the beach to see your ship, and I could not see it. I wept, then, till the night, telling myself continually, "Teriitera returns into his own country and leaves his dear Rui in grief, so that I suffer for him, and weep for him." I will not forget you in my memory. Here is the thought: I desire to meet you again. It is my dear Teriitera makes the only riches I desire in this world. It is your eyes that I desire to see again. It must be that your body and my body shall eat together at our table: there is what would make my heart content. But now we are separated. May God be with you all. May His word and His mercy go with you, so that you may be well and we also, according to the words of Paul.

ORI A ORI; that is to say, RUI.

After reading this to me Louis has left in tears saying that he is not worthy that such a letter should be written to him. We hope to so manage that we shall stop at Tahiti and see Rui once more. I tell myself that pleasant story when I wake in the night.

I find my head swimming so that I cannot write any more. I wish some rich Catholic would send a parlor organ to Père Bruno of Tautira. I am going to try and save money to do it myself, but he may die before I have enough. I feel ashamed to be sitting here when I think of that old man who cannot draw because of scrivener's paralysis, who has no one, year in and year out, to speak to but natives (our Rui is a Protestant, not bigoted like the rest of them—but still a Protestant) and the only pastime he has is playing on an old broken parlor organ whose keys are mostly dumb. I know no more pathetic figure. Have you no rich Catholic friends who would send him an organ that he could play upon? Of course I am talking nonsense, and yet I know somewhere that person exists if only I knew the place.

Our dearest love to you all.
FANNY

LETTERS FROM HAWAII

8. To Henry James

When Henry James (1843–1916), famed American novelist and expatriate, published in 1884 his volume of criticism, The Art of Fiction, *R.L.S. responded by publishing "A Humble Remonstrance." Continued mutual concern with the author's craft resulted in cordial visits by James to the Stevenson household at Bournemouth in the spring of 1885. Thereafter the two writers corresponded until Stevenson's death.*

Honolulu [March 1889]

MY DEAR JAMES,

Yes—I own up—I am untrue to friendship and (what is less, but still considerable) to civilization. I am not coming home for another year. There it is, cold and bald, and now you won't believe in me at all, and serve me right (says you) and the devil take me. But look here, and judge me tenderly. I have had more fun and pleasure of my life these past months than ever before, and more health than any time in ten long years. And even here in Honolulu I have withered in the cold; and this precious deep is filled with islands, which we may still visit; and though the sea is a deathful place, I like to be there, and like squalls (when they are over) ; and to draw near to a new island, I cannot say how much I like. In short, I take another year of this sort of life, and mean to try to work down among the poisoned arrows, and mean (if it may be) to come back again when the thing is through, and converse with Henry James as heretofore; and in the meanwhile issue directions to H.J. to write to me once more. Let him address here at Honolulu, for my views are vague; and if it is sent here it will follow and find me, if I am to be found; and if I am not to be found, the man James will have done his duty, and we shall be at the bottom of the sea, where no post-office clerk can be expected to discover us, or languishing on a coral island, the philosophic drudges of some barbarian potentate: perchance, of an American missionary. My wife has just sent to Mrs. Sitwell a translation (*tant bien que mal*) of a letter I have had from my chief friend [Ori a Ori, or Rui, of Tahiti] in this part of the world: go and see her, and get a hearing of it; it will do you good; it is a better method of correspondence than even Henry James'. I jest, but seriously it is a strange thing for a tough, sick, middle-aged scrivener like R.L.S. to receive a letter so conceived from a man fifty years old, a leading politician, a crack orator, and the great wit of his village: boldly say, "the highly popular M.P. of Tautira." My nineteenth century strikes here, and lies alongside of something beautiful and ancient. I think the receipt of such a letter might humble, shall I say even ————? and for me, I would rather have received it than written *Redgauntlet* or the sixth *Æneid*. All told, if my books have enabled or helped me to make this voyage, to know Rui, and to have received such a letter, they have (in the old prefatorial expression) not been writ in vain. It would seem from this that I have been not so much humbled as puffed up; but, I assure you, I have in fact been both. A little of what that letter says is my own earning; not all, but yet a little; and the little makes me proud, and all the rest ashamed; and in the contrast, how much more beautiful altogether is the ancient man than him of today!

Well, well, Henry James is pretty good, though he *is* of the nineteenth century, and that glaringly. And to curry favor with him, I wish I could be more explicit; but, indeed, I am still of necessity extremely vague, and cannot tell what I am to do, nor where I am to go for some while yet. As soon as I am sure, you shall hear. All are fairly well—the wife, your countrywoman, least of all; troubles are not entirely wanting; but on the whole we prosper, and we are all affectionately yours,

ROBERT LOUIS STEVENSON

9. TO SIDNEY COLVIN

Honolulu, April 2nd, 1889

MY DEAR COLVIN,

I am beginning to be ashamed of writing on to you without the least acknowledgment, like a tramp; but I do not care—I am hardened; and whatever be the cause of your silence, I mean to write till all is blue. I am outright ashamed of my news, which is that we are not coming home for another year. I cannot but hope it may continue the vast improvement of my health: I think it good for Fanny and Lloyd; and we have all a taste for this wandering and dangerous life. My mother I send home, to my relief, as this part of our cruise will be (if we can carry it out) rather difficult in places. Here is the idea: about the middle of June (unless the Boston Board objects) we sail from Honolulu in the missionary ship (barkentine auxiliary steamer) *Morning Star*: she takes us through the Gilberts and Marshalls, and drops us (this is my great idea) on Ponape, one of the volcanic islands of the Carolines. Here we stay marooned among a doubtful population, with a Spanish vice-governor and five native kings, and a sprinkling of missionaries all at loggerheads, on the chance of fetching a passage to Sydney in a trader, a labor ship or (maybe, but this appears too bright) a ship of war. If we can't get the *Morning Star* (and the Board has many reasons that I can see for refusing its permission) I mean to try to fetch Fiji, hire a schooner there, do the Fijis and Friendlies, hit the course of the *Richmond* at Tongatabu, make back by Tahiti, and so to S.F., and home: perhaps in June 1890. For the latter part of the cruise will likely be the same in either case. You can see for yourself how much variety and adventure this promises, and that it is not devoid of danger at the best; but if we can pull it off in safety, gives me a fine book of travel, and Lloyd a fine lecture and diorama, which should vastly better our finances.

I feel as if I were untrue to friendship; believe me, Colvin, when I look forward to this absence of another year, my conscience sinks at thought of the Monument: but I think you will pardon me if you consider how much this tropical weather mends my health. Remember me as I was at home, and think of me sea bathing and walking about, as jolly as a sandboy: you will own the temptation is strong; and as the scheme, bar fatal accidents, is bound to pay into the bargain, sooner or later, it seems it would be madness to come home now, with an imperfect book, no illustrations to speak of, no diorama, and perhaps fall sick again by autumn. I do not think I delude myself when I say the tendency to catarrh has visibly diminished.

It is a singular thing that as I was packing up old papers ere I left Skerryvore, I came on the prophecies of a drunken Highland sibyl, when I was seventeen. She said I was to be very happy, to visit America, and *to be much upon the sea*. It seems as if it were coming true with a vengeance. Also, do you remember my strong, old, rooted belief that I shall die by drowning? I don't want that to come true, though it is an easy death; but it occurs to me oddly, with these long chances in front. I cannot say why I like the sea; no man is more cynically and constantly alive to its perils; I regard it as the highest form of gambling; and yet I love the sea as much as I hate gambling. Fine, clean emotions; a world all and always beautiful; air better than wine; interest unflagging; there is upon the whole no better life.—Yours ever,

R.L.S.

10. To E. L. Burlingame

Stevenson had become accustomed to asking the editor of Scribner's Magazine *to send him books that might be needed in his work. R.L.S. here, fulfilling the fears of his wife that he might be tempted to imitate Frederick Marryat and other writers inferior to him, is ordering a miscellany of volumes before embarking for the southern Pacific islands.*

TRAVELS IN HAWAII

MY DEAR BURLINGAME,

This is to announce the most prodigious change of program. I have seen so much of the South Seas that I desire to see more, and I get so much health here that I dread a return to our vile climates. I have applied accordingly to the missionary folk to let me go round in the *Morning Star*; and if the Boston Board should refuse, I shall get somehow to Fiji, hire a trading schooner, and see the Fijis and Friendlies and Samoa. He would be a South Seayer, Mr. Burlingame. Of course, if I go in the *Morning Star,* I see all the eastern (or western?) islands.

Before I sail, I shall make out to let you have the last of *The Master*: though I tell you it sticks!—and I hope to have had some proofs forbye, of the verses anyway. And now to business.

I want (if you can find them) in the British sixpenny edition, if not, in some equally compact and portable shape—Seaside Library, for instance—the Waverley Novels entire, or as entire as you can get 'em, and the following of Marryat: *Phantom Ship, Peter Simple, Percival Keene, Privateersman, Children of the New Forest, Frank Mildmay, Newton Forster, Dog Fiend* (*Snarleyyow*). Also *Midshipman Easy, Kingsburn,* Carlyle's *French Revolution,* Motley's *Dutch Republic,* Lang's *Letters on Literature,* a complete set of my works, *Jenkin,* in duplicate; also *Familiar Studies,* ditto.

I have to thank you for the accounts, which are satisfactory indeed, and for the check for $1,000. Another account will have come and gone before I see you. I hope it will be equally roseate in color.

I am quite worked out, and this cursed end of *The Master* hangs over me like the arm of the gallows; but it is always darkest before dawn, and no doubt the clouds will soon rise; but it is a difficult thing to write, above all in Mackellarese; and I cannot yet see my way clear. If I pull this off, *The Master* will be a pretty good novel or I am the more deceived; and even if I don't pull it off, it'll still have some stuff in it.

We shall remain here until the middle of June anyway; but my mother leaves for Europe early in May. Hence our mail should continue to come here; but not hers. I will let you know my next address, which will probably be Sydney. If we get on the *Morning Star,* I propose at present to get marooned on Ponape, and take my chance of getting a passage to Australia. It will leave times and seasons mighty vague, and the cruise is risky; but I shall know something of the South Seas when it is done, or else the South Seas will contain all there is of me. It should give me a fine book of travels, anyway.

Low will probably come and ask some dollars of you. Pray let him have them, they are for outfit. O, another complete set of my books should go to Captain A. H. Otis, care of Dr. Merritt, Yacht *Casco,* Oakland, Cal.—In haste,

R.L.S.

11. To Miss Adelaide Boodle

Miss Boodle, a young friend of Bournemouth and Sker-ryvore days, had occasionally looked after things for the Stevensons. R.L.S. nicknamed her the "Gamekeeper" and

*himself the "Squire." Previously he had written to thank
her for the gift of a paper cutter.*

Honolulu, April 6th, 1889

MY DEAR MISS BOODLE,

Nobody writes a better letter than my Game-keeper: so gay, so pleasant, so engagingly particular, answering (by some delicate instinct) all the questions she suggests. It is a shame you should get such a poor return as I can make, from a mind essentially and originally incapable of the art epistolary. I would let the paper cutter take my place; but I am sorry to say the little wooden seaman did after the manner of seamen, and deserted in the Societies. The place he seems to have stayed at—seems, for his absence was not observed till we were near the Equator —was Tautira, and, I assure you, he displayed good taste, Tautira being as "nigh hand heaven" as a paper cutter or anybody has a right to expect.

I think all our friends will be very angry with us, and I give the grounds of their probable displeasure bluntly—we are not coming home for another year. My mother returns next month. Fanny, Lloyd, and I push on again among the islands on a trading schooner, the *Equator*—first for the Gilbert group, which we shall have an opportunity to explore thoroughly; then, if occasion serve, to the Marshalls and Carolines; and if occasion (or money) fail, to Samoa, and back to Tahiti. I own we are deserters, but we have excuses. You cannot conceive how these climates agree with the wretched houseplant of Skerryvore: he wonders to find himself sea bathing, and cutting about the world loose, like a grown-up person. They agree with Fanny too, who does not suffer from her rheumatism, and with Lloyd also. And the interest of the islands is endless; and the sea, though I own it is a fearsome place, is very delightful. We had applied for places in the American missionary ship, the *Morning Star,* but this trading schooner is a far preferable idea, giving us more time and a thousandfold more liberty, so we determined to cut off the missionaries with a shilling.

The Sandwich Islands do not interest us very much; we live here, oppressed with civilization, and look for good things in the future. But it would surprise you if you came out tonight from Honolulu (all shining with electric lights, and all in a bustle from the arrival of the mail, which is to carry you these lines) and crossed the long wooden causeway along the beach, and came out on the road through Kapiolani Park, and seeing a gate in the palings, with a tub of goldfish by the wayside, entered casually in. The buildings stand in three groups by the edge of the beach, where an angry little spitfire sea continually spirts and thrashes with impotent irascibility, the big seas breaking further out upon the reef. The first is a small house, with a very large summer parlor, or lanai, as they call it here, roofed, but practically open. There you will find the lamps burning and the family sitting about the table, dinner just done: my mother, my wife, Lloyd, Belle, my wife's daughter, Austin her child, and tonight (by way of rarity) a guest. All about the walls our South Sea curiosities, war clubs, idols, pearl shells, stone axes, etc.; and the walls are only a small part of a lanai, the rest being glazed or latticed windows, or mere open space. You will see there no sign of the Squire, however; and being a person of a humane disposition, you will only glance in over the balcony railing at the merrymakers in the summer parlor, and proceed further afield after the exile. You look round, there is beautiful green turf, many trees of an outlandish sort that drop thorns—look out if your feet are bare; but I beg your pardon, you have not been long enough in the South Seas—and many oleanders in full flower. The next group of buildings is ramshackle, and quite dark; you make out a coach-house door, and look in—only some coconuts; you try round to the left and come to the sea front, where Venus and the moon are making luminous tracks on the water, and a great swell rolls and shines on the outer reef; and here is another door—all these places open from the outside—and you go in, and find photography, tubs of water, negatives steeping, a tap, and a chair and an ink bottle, where my wife is supposed to write; round a little further, a third door, entering which you find a picture upon the easel and a table sticky with paints; a fourth door admits you to a sort of court, where there is a hen sitting—I believe on a fallacious egg. No sign of the Squire in all this. But right opposite the studio door you have observed a third little house, from whose open door lamplight streams and makes hay of the strong moonlight shadows. You had supposed it made no part of the grounds, for a fence runs round it lined with oleander; but as the Squire is nowhere else, is it not just possible he may be here? It is a grim little wooden shanty; cobwebs bedeck it; friendly mice inhabit its recesses; the mailed cockroach walks upon the wall;

so also, I regret to say, the scorpion. Herein are two pallet beds, two mosquito curtains, strung to the pitch-boards of the roof, two tables laden with books and manuscripts, three chairs, and, in one of the beds, the Squire busy writing to yourself, as it chances, and just at this moment, somewhat bitten by mosquitoes. He has just set fire to the insect powder, and will be all right in no time; but just now he contemplates large white blisters, and would like to scratch them, but knows better. The house is not bare; it has been inhabited by kanakas, and—you know what children are!—the bare wood walls are pasted over with pages from the *Graphic, Harper's Weekly,* etc. The floor is matted, and I am bound to say the matting is filthy. There are two windows and two doors, one of which is condemned; on the panels of that last a sheet of paper is pinned up, and covered with writing. I cull a few plums:—

"A duck hammock for each person.
A patent organ like the commandant's at Taiohae.
Cheap and bad cigars for presents.
Revolvers.
Permanganate of potash.
Liniment for the head and sulphur.
Fine tooth comb."

What do you think this is? Simply life in the South Seas foreshortened. These are a few of our desiderata for the next trip, which we jot down as they occur.

There, I have really done my best and tried to send something like a letter—one letter in return for all your dozens. Pray remember us all to yourself, Mrs. Boodle, and the rest of your house. I do hope your mother will be better when this comes. I shall write and give you a new address when I have made up my mind as to the most probable, and I do beg you will continue to write from time to time and give us airs from home. Tomorrow—think of it—I must be off by a quarter to eight to drive in to the palace and breakfast with His Hawaiian Majesty at 8 :30. I shall be dead indeed. Please give my news to Scott, I trust he is better; give him my warm regards. To you we all send all kinds of things, and I am the absentee Squire,

ROBERT LOUIS STEVENSON

12. TO CHARLES BAXTER

Honolulu, April 12th, 1889

MY DEAR CHARLES,

As usual your letter is as good as a cordial, and I thank you for it, and all your care, kindness, and generous and thoughtful friendship, from my heart. I was truly glad to hear a word of Colvin, whose long silence has terrified me; and glad to hear that you condoned the notion of my staying longer in the South Seas, for I have decided in that sense. The first idea was to go in the *Morning Star,* missionary ship, but now I have found a trading schooner, the *Equator,* which is to call for me here early (*D.V.*) in June, and carry us through the Gilberts. What will happen then, the Lord knows. My mother does not accompany us; she leaves here for home early in May, and you will hear of us from her, but not I imagine anything more definite. We shall get dumped on Butaritari, and whether we manage to go on to

the Marshalls and Carolines, or whether we fall back
on Samoa, Heaven must decide; but I mean to fetch
back into the course of the *Richmond* (to think you
don't know what the *Richmond* is!—*the* steamer of
the eastern South Seas, joining New Zealand, Tongatabu, the Samoas, Tahiti, and Rarotonga, and carrying, by last advices, sheep in the saloon!)—into the
course of the *Richmond* and make Tahiti once again
on the home track. I take my backgoing son-in-law
[Joseph Strong] along with me. This family has been
a sore trouble to me, but Joe is a good photographer,
and the idea is to get up a diorama and let Lloyd
lecture, and try to start a little money, honestly got,
for this Skimpolian household. Joe is a loveable fellow, but I tell you, and you know, I would rather
have to deal with D. A. Stevenson (in view of your
last news) or Paganini MacKnight than one of these
truculent fools who do not know the meaning of
money. It is heartbreaking; but there—the burthen
is on the back, and the diorama is an honest and hopeful pitch to lighten it. What think ye?

The picture of the chatelaine passing away in a
dwam of maternal vanity over what strikes me as a
portly and really personable infant has been going
round the family all evening (the steamer came in
but an hour or two ago) with rapture. A more dramatic work I never saw; and though it's the kind of
thing that tempts a man to chaff, it did my heart
good. Long may the babe flourish! And to think of it
in South Howard Place! I was born in plain Howard
Place, with none of the points of the compass, myself,
and it did my business. I wonder: I have always had
a little fear of that corner of Edinburgh; Warriston

Park is raither a Boggy Bit, isn't it not, Mr. John-s'one? or üsed to be?

Would I like to see the *Scots Observer*? Wouldn't I not? But whaur? I'm direckit at space. They have nae Post Offishes at the Gilberts, and as for the Car'lines! Ye see, Mr. Baxter, we're no just in the punkshewal center o' civ'lization. But pile them up for me, and when I've decided on a address, I'll let you ken, and ye'll can send them stavin' after me.

A propos of D. and T.S., I hear this with miserable feelings. It is a wretched business; I pray God it may not go so far as a case. If I were the only person to consider, I could cry quits now, rather than so damned a scandal should smirch my name; but of course I have no right to interfere with my mother, and no will to cut up what is the hope of all the family as well as of my folk; for I guess the Alans will get nothing from that crew, and they will always take something under my testament.

O—and another thing. As to the Young debt. It was never intended to chivvy Young, and if he has left his family in difficulties, neither my mother nor I would like the family chivvied. Pray deal with them in all gentleness.

You will keep up my charities please this year as last: the Xmas boxes and sich, and I have told Miss Boodle to apply to you in case the Watts family come to remediable grief. Act for me *tanquam Bonus P.F.* as usual; also *Bonus* P.D., or painful doer.

You shall hear from me again by next mail, I hope with clearer details. And I am meanwhile,

Ever your affectionate

R.L.S.

LETTERS FROM HAWAII

13. To Charles Baxter

Written presumably on April 25, eve of Stevenson's departure for the Kona Coast of Hawaii, this letter states what was apparently common knowledge—that King Kalākaua sought a treasure presumably hidden in one of the many caves there by Kamehameha I. It is unlikely that the latter ever sold gin to any pirates. Seldom noted is the episode in which the English and the American blue-jackets in Honolulu, united by a common bond after the hurricane at Samoa, spontaneously returned from church arm in arm. This letter, omitted by Colvin, is reprinted, by the kind permission of Yale University Press, from R.L.S.: Stevenson's Letters to Charles Baxter, *ed. De-Lancey Ferguson and Marshall Waingrow, New Haven, 1956, pp. 246–247.*

[Honolulu, April 25th, 1889]

MY DEAR CHARLES,

I forget if I have made my plans clear to you. They stand thus:

We should leave Honolulu early in June, per trading schooner *Equator* for the Gilbert Islands. Our subsequent movements, which are quite in the air, will be most briefly indicated by this post office guide: Letters: c/o H.B.M. Consul, Apia, Samoa, "to await arrival" up to September inclusive; c/o H.B.M. Consul, Papeete, Tahiti, "to await arrival" up to December inclusive; c/o E. B. Young, S.F., Cal., thereafter.

I wish you would register the title *The Pearlfisher* [later *The Ebb-Tide*] for me. It is for a story Lloyd and I are on—the gaudiest yarn—and I have a dreadful fear someone will burk the name, as has happened to me once before with *Robin Run-the-Hedge.*

I am off work and go to Hawaii for ten days for a change, to a home of the King's; he says one man can speak English. It is on the Kona Coast, where the King is perpetually engaged on a treasure chase. Old Kamehameha the 1st (or 2nd, I forget which) sold gin to the pirates, and his female chamberlains buried the proceeds in a cave upon that seaboard; but alas! there are many hundred caverns there, and the chamberlains died game. Hence, *sa majesté actuelle revient* and *reviendra toujours bredouille.*

A pretty touch of seaman manners: the English and American Jacks are deadly rivals. Well, after all this hammering of both sides by the Germans, and then the news of the hurricane from Samoa, a singular scene occurred Sunday before last. The two church parties, *sponte propria,* fell in line together, one Englishman to one American, and marched down to the harbor side like one ship's company. None were more surprised than their own officers. I have seen a hantle of the seaman on this cruise; I always liked him before; my first crew on the *Casco* (five sea lawyers) near cured me; but I have returned to my first love.

I must say farewell, as the night draws on and I must be on "the eight seas" tomorrow.

Ever yours,
R. L. STEVENSON

14. To CHARLES BAXTER

The first paragraph of this letter refers to the publication in the press, which Baxter had allowed, of one of Stevenson's letters written earlier in the voyage. R.L.S., who disliked the publication of private letters during the writer's lifetime, had remonstrated; and now writes to soften the effect of his remonstrance.

Honolulu, May 10th, 1889

MY DEAR CHARLES,

I am appalled to gather from your last just to hand that you have felt so much concern about the letter. Pray dismiss it from your mind. But I think you scarce appreciate how disagreeable it is to have your private affairs and private unguarded expressions getting into print. It would soon sicken anyone of writing letters. I have no doubt that letter was very wisely selected, but it just shows how things crop up: there was a raging jealousy between the two yachts, our captain was nearly in a fight over it. However, no more; and whatever you think, my dear fellow, do not suppose me angry with you or Coggie; although I was *annoyed at the circumstance*—a very different thing. But it is hard to conduct life by letter, and I continually feel I may be drifting into some matter of offense, in which my heart takes no part. Please reassure Coggie.

I must now turn to a point of business. This new cruise of ours is somewhat venturesome, and I think it needful to warn you not to be in a hurry to suppose us dead. In these ill-charted seas, it is quite on the cards we might be cast on some unvisited or very rarely visited island; that there we might lie for a long time, even years, unheard of, and yet turn up smiling at the hinder end. So do not let me be "row-pit" [sold at auction], till you get some certainty we have gone to Davie Jones in a squall or graced the feast of some barbarian in the character of long pig.

I have at last heard from Colvin; he must have had a real bad turn. I gather I have had a touch of the same; overwork brought on a very distressing attack of blood to the head, so that I could scarcely see, scarcely understand what was said to me, and presented by way of face a purple expanse only enlivened by a pair of white lips. I trust mine has drifted off without further harm. I hope [Jean Martin] Charcot will get him round. I will back you up, of course, as I have said so often, in anything it may be possible to do for him. It is already cheering we have been able to do something.

I have just been a week away alone on the lee coast of Hawaii; the only white creature in many miles, riding five and a half hours one day, living with a native, seeing poor lepers shipped off to Molokai, hearing native causes and giving my opinion as *amicus curiae* as to the interpretation of a statute in English: a lovely week among God's best—at least God's sweetest—works, Polynesians. It has bettered me greatly. If I could only stay there the time that remains, I could get my work done and be happy; but the care of a large, costly, and no' just preceesely forrit-gaun family keeps me in vile Honolulu, where I am always out of sorts, amidst heat and cold and cesspools and beastly haoles. What is a haole? You are one, and so, I am sorry to say, am I. After so long a dose of whites, it was a blessing to get among Polynesians again, even for a week.

Weel Charles, there are waur haoles than yoursel', I'll say that for ye; and I trust before I sail, I shall get another letter in a vein of more content and with more about yourself.

Ever your affectionate friend,
R.L.S.

It is strange to think: during all these months when I have been in postal range, till this letter of Colvin, you are the only one of my old friends who has written to me. When I seemed to feel in your last that you too were a little irritated, this came home to me sharply. I see partly where I have been to blame; yet I think it is rather hard measure; and perhaps if you will consider this isolation, and how very annoying it is never to be able to write a careless word lest it should find its way into the newspapers, you will be inclined to make more allowance.

15. To W. H. Low

Will Hicok Low (1853–1932), whom R.L.S. first met at an artist's colony near Paris in 1875, was an American painter and illustrator. Stevenson corresponded with him frequently during his lifetime. The latter half of the letter here alludes to the departure of Princess Ka'iulani and to the American Rear Admiral Kimberley, whose men, during their doomed fight against the hurricane at Apia, Samoa, cheered on the escaping vessel H.M.S. Calliope.

TRAVELS IN HAWAII

MY DEAR LOW,

. . . I have at length finished *The Master*; it has been a sore cross to me; but now he is buried, his body's under hatches,—his soul, if there is any hell to go to, gone to hell; and I forgive him: it is harder to forgive Burlingame for having induced me to begin the publication, or myself for suffering the induction.—Yes, I think Hole has done finely; it will be one of the most adequately illustrated books of our generation; he gets the note, he tells the story—*my* story: I know only one failure—the Master standing on the beach.—You must have a letter for me at Sydney—till further notice. Remember me to Mrs. Will, H., the godlike sculptor, and any of the faithful. If you want to cease to be a republican, see my little Ka'iulani, as she goes through—but she is gone already. You will die a red: I wear the colors of that little royal maiden, *Nous allons chanter à la ronde, si vous voulez!* only she is not blonde by several chalks, though she is but a half-blood, and the wrong half Edinburgh Scots like mysel'. But, O Low, I love the Polynesian: this civilization of ours is a dingy, ungentlemanly business; it drops out too much of man, and too much of that the very beauty of the poor beast; who has his beauties in spite of Zola and Co. As usual, here is a whole letter with no news: I am a bloodless, inhuman dog; and no doubt Zola is a better correspondent.—Long live your fine old English admiral—yours, I mean—the U.S.A. one at Samoa; I wept tears and loved myself and mankind when I read of him: he is not too much civilized. And there was [Charles George?] Gordon, too; and there are others, beyond question. But if you could live, the only white folk, in a Polynesian village; and drink that warm, light *vin du pays* of human affection and enjoy that simple dignity of all about you— I will not gush, for I am now in my fortieth year, which seems highly unjust, but there it is, Mr. Low, and the Lord enlighten your affectionate

R.L.S.

16. FROM MRS. R. L. STEVENSON TO SIDNEY COLVIN

Fanny Stevenson, in her role as hearthside critic of the working plans of her husband, here urges Colvin to divert the grand design of R.L.S. to do a factual volume on the South Seas, drawing upon other authors.

Honolulu, May 21st, 1889

BEST OF FRIENDS,

It was a joy inexpressible to get a word from you at last. Fortunately for our peace of mind, we were almost positive that your letters had been sent to the places we had already left. Still it was a bitter disappointment to get nothing from you when we arrived here. I wish you could have seen us both throwing over the immense package of letters searching for your handwriting. Now that we know you have been ill, please do let someone send us a line to our next address telling us how you are. What that next address may be we do not yet know, as our final movements are a little uncertain. To begin with, a trading schooner, the *Equator,* will come along sometime in the first part of June, lie outside the harbor here and signal to us. Within forty-eight hours we shall pack up our possessions, our barrel of sauerkraut, our barrel of salt onions, our bag of coconuts, our native garments, our tobacco, fishhooks, red combs, and Turkey red calicoes (all the latter for trading purposes), our hand organ, photograph and painting materials, and finally our magic lantern—all these upon a large whaleboat, and go out to the *Equator*. Lloyd, also, takes a fiddle, a guitar, a native instrument something like a banjo, called a taropatch fiddle [ukulele], and a lot of songbooks. We shall be carried first to one of the Gilberts, landing at Butaritari. The *Equator* is going about among the Gilbert group, and we have the right to keep her over when we like within reasonable limits. Finally she will leave us, and we shall have to take the chances of what happens next. We hope to see the Marshalls, the Carolines, the Fijis, Tonga, and Samoa (also other islands that I do not remember), perhaps staying a little while in Sydney, and stopping on our way home to see our friends in Tahiti and the Marquesas. I am very much exercised by one thing. Louis has the most enchanting material that any one ever had in the whole world for his book, and I am afraid he is going to spoil it all. He has taken into his Scotch Stevenson head that a stern duty lies before him, and that his book must be a sort of scientific and historical impersonal thing, comparing the different languages (of which he knows nothing, really) and the different peoples, the object being to settle the question as to whether they are of common Malay origin or not. Also to compare the Protestant and Catholic missions, etc., and the whole thing to be impersonal, leaving out all he knows of the people themselves. And I believe there is no one living who has got so near to them, or who understands them as he does. Think of a small treatise on the Polynesian races being offered to people who are dying to hear about Ori a Ori, the making of brothers with cannibals, the strange stories they told, and the extraordinary adventures that befell us:— suppose Herman Melville had given us his theories as to the Polynesian language and the probable good or evil results of the missionary influence instead of *Omoo* and *Typee,* or [Henry] Kinglake [omission] instead of *Eothen.* Louis says it is a stern sense of duty that is at the bottom of it, which is more alarming than anything else. I am so sure that you will agree with me that I am going to ask you to throw the weight of your influence as heavily as possible in the scales with me. Please refer to the matter in the letters we shall receive at our first stopping place, otherwise Louis will spend a great deal of time in Sydney actually reading up other people's books on the Islands. What a thing it is to have a "man of genius" to deal with. It is like managing an overbred horse. Why, with my own feeble hand I could write a book that the whole world would jump at. Please keep any letters of mine that contain any incidents of our wanderings. They are very exact as to facts, and Louis may, in this conscientious state of mind (indeed I am afraid he has), put nothing in his diary but statistics. Even if I thought it a desirable thing to write what he proposes, I should still think it impossible unless after we had lived and studied here some twenty years or more.

Now I am done with my complaining, and shall

turn to the pleasanter paths. Louis went to one of the other islands a couple of weeks ago, quite alone, got drenched with rain and surf, rode over mountain paths—five and a half hours one day—and came back none the worse for it. Today he goes to Molokai, the leper island. He never has a sign of hemorrhage, the air cushion is a thing of the past, and altogether he is a new man. How he will do in the English climate again I do not know, but in these latitudes he is very nearly a well man; nothing seems to do him harm but overwork. That, of course, is sometimes difficult to prevent. Now, however, the *Master* is done, we have enough money to go upon and there is no need to work at all. I must stop. My dear love to you all.

FANNY V. DE G. STEVENSON

17. TO MRS. R. L. STEVENSON

The following letter, written on the evening of R.L.S.'s arrival at the leper colony, gives a view of his first impressions of the steamer trip and his arrival at Kalawao, and shows as well his disappointment at not being able to ascend the precipice dividing the peninsula from the rest of Molokai.

Kalawao, Molokai [May 1889]

DEAR FANNY,

I had a lovely sail up. Captain Cameron and Mr. Gilfillan [the purser], both born in the States, yet the first still with a strong Highland, and the second still with a strong Lowland, accent were good company; the night was warm, the victuals plain but good. Mr. Gilfillan gave me his berth, and I slept well, though I heard the sisters [two Catholic nuns] sick in the next stateroom, poor souls. Heavy rolling woke me in the morning; I turned in all standing, so went right on the upper deck. The day was on the peep out of a low morning bank, and we were wallowing along under stupendous cliffs. As the lights brightened, we could see certain abutments and buttresses on their front where wood clustered and grass grew brightly. But the whole brow seemed quite impassable, and my heart sank at the sight. Two thousand feet of rock making nineteen degrees (the captain guesses) seemed quite beyond my powers. However, I had come so far; and, to tell you the truth, I was so cowed with fear and disgust that I dared not go back on the adventure in the interests of my own self-respect. Presently we came up with the leper promontory: lowland, quite bare and bleak and harsh, a little town of wooden houses, two churches, a landing stair, all unsightly, sour, northerly, lying athwart the sunrise, with the great wall of the pali cutting the world out on the south. Our lepers were sent on the first boat, about a dozen, one poor child very horrid, one white man, leaving a large grown family behind him in Honolulu, and then into the second stepped the sisters and myself. I do not know how it would have been with me had the sisters not been there. My horror of the horrible is about my weakest point; but the moral loveliness at my elbow blotted all else out; and when I found that one of them was crying, poor soul, quietly under her veil, I cried a little myself; then I felt as right as a trivet, only a little crushed to be there so uselessly. I thought it was a sin and a shame she should feel unhappy; I turned round to her, and said something like this: "Ladies, God Himself is here to give you welcome. I'm sure it is good for me to be beside you; I hope it will be blessed to me; I thank you for myself and the good you do me." It seemed to cheer her up; but indeed I had scarce said it when we were at the landing stairs, and there was a great crowd, hundreds of (God save us!) pantomime masks in poor human flesh, waiting to receive the sisters and the new patients.

Every hand was offered: I had gloves, but I had made up my mind on the boat's voyage *not* to give my hand; that seemed less offensive than the gloves. So the sisters and I went up among that crew, and presently I got aside (for I felt I had no business there) and set off on foot across the promontory, carrying my wrap and the camera. All horror was quite gone from me: to see these dread creatures smile and look happy was beautiful. On my way through Kalaupapa I was exchanging cheerful alohas with the patients coming galloping over on their horses; I was stopping to gossip at house doors; I was happy, only ashamed of myself that I was here for no good. One woman was pretty, and spoke good English, and was infinitely engaging and (in the old phrase) towardly; she thought I was the new white patient; and when she found I was only a visitor, a curious change came in her face and voice —the only sad thing, morally sad, I mean—that I met that morning. But for all that, they tell me none want to leave. Beyond Kalaupapa the houses became rare; dry stone dykes, grassy, stony land, one sick pandanus; a dreary country; from overhead in the little clinging wood shogs of the pali chirruping of birds fell; the low sun was right in my face; the trade blew pure and cool and delicious; I felt as right as ninepence, and stopped and chatted with the patients whom I still met on their horses, with not the least disgust. About halfway over, I met the superintendent (a leper) with a horse for me, and O, wasn't I glad! But the horse was one of those curious, dogged, cranky brutes that always dully want to go somewhere else, and my traffic with him completed my crushing fatigue. I got to the guest-house, an empty house with several rooms, kitchen, bath, etc. There was no one there, and I let the horse go loose in the garden, lay down on the bed, and fell asleep.

Dr. Swift woke me and gave me breakfast, then I came back and slept again while he was at the dispensary, and he woke me for dinner; and I came back and slept again, and he woke me about six for supper; and then in about an hour I felt tired again, and came up to my solitary guesthouse, played the flageolet, and am now writing to you. As yet, you see, I have seen nothing of the settlement, and my crushing fatigue (though I believe that was moral and a measure of my cowardice) and the doctor's opinion make me think the pali hopeless. "You don't look a strong man," said the doctor; "but are you sound?" I told him the truth; then he said it was out of the question, and if I were to get up at all, I must be carried up. But, as it seems, men as well as horses continually fall on this ascent: the doctor goes up with a change of clothes—it is plain that to be carried would in itself be very fatiguing to both mind and body; and I should then be at the beginning of thirteen miles of mountain road to be ridden against time. How should I come through? I hope you will think me right in my decision: I mean to stay, and shall not be back in Honolulu till Saturday, June first. You must all do the best you can to make ready.

Dr. Swift has a wife and an infant son, beginning to toddle and run, and they live here as composed as brick and mortar—at least the wife does, a Kentucky German, a fine enough creature, I believe, who was quite amazed at the sisters' shedding tears! How strange is mankind! Gilfillan too, a good fellow I think, and far from stupid, kept up his hard Lowland Scottish talk in the boat while the sister was covering her face; but I believe he knew, and did it (partly) in embarrassment, and part perhaps in mistaken kindness. And that was one reason, too, why I made my speech to them. Partly, too, I did it, because I was ashamed to do so, and remembered one of my golden rules, "When you are ashamed to speak, speak up at once." But, mind you, that rule is only golden with strangers; with your own folks, there are other considerations. This is a strange place to be in. A bell has been sounded at intervals while I wrote, now all is still but a musical humming of the sea, not unlike the sound of telegraph wires; the night is quite cool and pitch dark, with a small fine rain; one light over in the leper settlement, one cricket whistling in the garden, my lamp here by my bedside, and my pen cheeping between my inky fingers.

Next day, lovely morning, slept all night, eighty degrees in the shade, strong, sweet Anaho trade wind.

LOUIS

LETTERS FROM HAWAII

18. To Sidney Colvin

R.L.S. here reports on his visit to Molokai, and gives his brief character sketch of Father Damien (see also Letter 22). He mentions also that he is going to interview the survivors of the wrecked schooner Wandering Minstrel.

Honolulu, June 1889

MY DEAR COLVIN,

I am just home after twelve days' journey to Molokai, seven of them at the leper settlement, where I can only say that the sight of so much courage, cheerfulness, and devotion strung me too high to mind the infinite pity and horror of the sights. I used to ride over from Kalawao to Kalaupapa (about three miles across the promontory, the cliff wall, ivied with forest and yet inaccessible from steepness, on my left), go to the sisters' home, which is a miracle of neatness, play a game of croquet with seven leper girls (ninety degrees in the shade), got a little old-maid meal served me by the sisters, and ride home again, tired enough, but not too tired. The girls all have dolls, and love dressing them. You who know so many ladies delicately clad, and they who know so many dressmakers, please make it known it would be an acceptable gift to send scraps for doll dressmaking to the Reverend Sister Maryanne, Bishop Home, Kalaupapa, Molokai, Hawaiian Islands.

I have seen sights that cannot be told, and heard stories that cannot be repeated: yet I never admired my poor race so much, nor (strange as it may seem) loved life more than in the settlement. A horror of

moral beauty broods over the place: that's like bad
Victor Hugo, but it is the only way I can express the
sense that lived with me all these days. And this even
though it was in great part Catholic, and my sym-
pathies flew never with so much difficulty as towards
Catholic virtues. The passbook kept with heaven
stirs me to anger and laughter. One of the sisters calls
the place "the ticket office to heaven." Well, what is
the odds? They do their darg [day's work], and do
it with kindness and efficiency incredible; and we
must take folks' virtues as we find them, and love
the better part. Of old Damien, whose weaknesses
and worse perhaps I heard fully, I think only the
more. It was a European peasant: dirty, bigoted,
untruthful, unwise, tricky, but superb with generosity, residual candor and fundamental good humor:
convince him he had done wrong (it might take
hours of insult) and he would undo what he had
done and like his corrector better. A man, with all
the grime and paltriness of mankind, but a saint
and hero all the more for that. The place as regards
scenery is grand, gloomy, and bleak. Mighty mountain walls descending sheer along the whole face of
the island into a sea unusually deep; the front of the
mountain ivied and furred with clinging forest, one
viridescent cliff: about halfway from east to west,
the low, bare, stony promontory edged in between
the cliff and the ocean; the two little towns (Kalawao and Kalaupapa) seated on either side of it, as
bare almost as bathing machines upon a beach; and
the population—gorgons and chimeras dire. All this
tear of the nerves I bore admirably; and the day after
I got away, rode twenty miles along the opposite

coast and up into the mountains: they call it twenty, I am doubtful of the figures: I should guess it nearer twelve; but let me take credit for what residents allege; and I was riding again the day after, so I need say no more about health. Honolulu does not agree with me at all: I am always out of sorts there, with slight headache, blood to the head, etc. I had a good deal of work to do and did it with miserable difficulty; and yet all the time I have been gaining strength, as you see, which is highly encouraging. By the time I am done with this cruise I shall have the material for a very singular book of travels: names of strange stories and characters, cannibals, pirates, ancient legends, old Polynesian poetry,— never was so generous a farrago. I am going down now to get the story of a shipwrecked family, who were fifteen months on an island with a murderer: there is a specimen. The Pacific is a strange place; the nineteenth century exists there only in spots: all round, it is a no man's land of the ages, a stirabout of epochs and races, barbarisms and civilizations, virtues and crimes.

It is good of you to let me stay longer, but if I had known how ill you were, I should be now on my way home. I had chartered my schooner and made all arrangements before (at last) we got definite news. I feel highly guilty; I should be back to insult and worry you a little. Our address till further notice is to be c/o R. Towns & Co., Sydney. That is final: I got the arrangement made only yesterday; but you may now publish it abroad.

Yours ever,
R.L.S.

19. To James Payn

R.L.S. herein reports to an old friend of Cornhill Magazine *days who, he had heard, was troubled by ill health
and increasing deafness.*

Honolulu, H.I., June 13th, 1889

MY DEAR JAMES PAYN,

I get sad news of you here at my offsetting for
further voyages: I wish I could say what I feel. Sure
there was never any man less deserved this calamity;
for I have heard you speak time and again, and I
remember nothing that was unkind, nothing that
was untrue, nothing that was not helpful, from your
lips. It is the ill talkers that should hear no more.
God knows, I know no word of consolation; but I
do feel your trouble. You are the more open to letters
now; let me talk to you for two pages. I have nothing
but happiness to tell; and you may bless God you are
a man so sound-hearted that (even in the freshness of
your calamity) I can come to you with my own good
fortune unashamed and secure of sympathy. It is a
good thing to be a good man, whether deaf or
whether dumb; and of all our fellow craftsmen
(whom yet they count a jealous race), I never knew
one but gave you the name of honesty and kindness:
come to think of it gravely, this is better than the
finest hearing. We are all on the march to deafness,
blindness, and all conceivable and fatal disabilities;
we shall not all get there with a report so good. My
good news is a health astonishingly reinstated. This
climate; these voyagings; these landfalls at dawn;

new islands peaking from the morning bank; new forested harbors; new passing alarms of squalls and surf; new interests of gentle natives,—the whole tale of my life is better to me than any poem.

I am fresh just now from the leper settlement of Molokai, playing croquet with seven leper girls, sitting and yarning with old, blind, leper beachcombers in the hospital, sickened with the spectacle of abhorrent suffering and deformation among the patients, touched to the heart by the sight of lovely and effective virtues in their helpers: no stranger time have I ever had, nor any so moving. I do not think it a little thing to be deaf, God knows, and God defend me from the same!—but to be a leper, or one of the self-condemned, how much more awful! and yet there's a way there also. "There are Molokais everywhere," said Mr. [Joseph] Dutton, Father Damien's dresser; you are but new landed in yours; and my dear and kind adviser, I wish you, with all my soul, that patience and courage which you will require. Think of me meanwhile on a trading schooner, bound for the Gilbert Islands, thereafter for the Marshalls, with a diet of fish and coconut before me; bound on a cruise of—well, of investigation to what islands we can reach, and to get (some day or other) to Sydney, where a letter addressed to the care of R. Towns & Co. will find me sooner or later; and if it contain any good news, whether of your welfare or the courage with which you bear the contrary, will do me good.

Yours affectionately (although so near a stranger),

ROBERT LOUIS STEVENSON

TRAVELS IN HAWAII

20. To Mrs. Thomas Stevenson

Another account of his visit to Molokai and of later events is given by R.L.S. to his mother, who had left on May 10 on her way to Scotland. This item, missing in the 1911 edition of the Letters, *was included in the 1923 edition, pp. 133–135.*

Honolulu, June 1889

MY DEAR MOTHER,

Herewith goes a copy of my first letter from the leper settlement; my second, that is to say my diary, is too long to copy, as it runs to near forty pages. I can only tell you briefly that I was a week in the settlement, hagridden by horrid sights but really inspired with the sight of so much goodness in the helpless and so much courage and unconsciousness in the sick. The Bishop Home (the sisters' place) is perfect. I went there most days to play croquet with the poor patients—think of a game of croquet with seven little lepers, and the thermometer sometimes ninety in the shade! I rode there and back, and used to have a little old-maid meal prepared for me alone by the sisters; and though I was often deadly tired, I was never the worse. The girls enjoyed the game a good deal, and the honor and glory of a clean haole gentleman for playmate yet more. They were none of them badly disfigured, but some of the bystanders were dreadful; but indeed I have seen sights to turn any man's hair white. The croquet helped me a bit, as I felt I was not quite doing nothing; Sister Mary-anne wanted me to sit down the second day, and only

tell the girls; I said, "they would not enjoy that."—
"Ah," said she, with a smiling eye, "you say that,
but the truth is you enjoy playing yourself!" And so
I did. When I came on board the *Mokoliʻi* (little
forty-ton steamer) to leave, I had no proper pass and
was refused entrance. I saw some very remarkable
fireworks, I can tell you, for I had had enough and
to spare of the distressful country. But it was all
made right; the captain took me ashore the same
evening at the north end of the island, gave me a
mount, introduced me to an innumerable Irish family
where I had supper and a bed, and gave me a horse
and a mounted guide next day, with whom I rode
twenty miles to Mr. Meyer's house. The next day,
I had another ride, a mighty rough drive over a kind
of road to the landing place; caught the *Mokoliʻi*
again, and was in Honolulu the morning after about
nine, very sunburnt and rudely well. How is that for
activity and rustic strength?

Grace is not invariable but (I may say) frequent;
and when not forgotten, is (ahem!) very well said.
Joe, Lloyd, and I are getting up music; guitar, taropatch [ukulele], flageolet, and voice for the show.
Le bon Damien is to give us a choice of his comic
slides; he has given us already a complete set of the
life of Christ; we have a fine magic lantern. Fu goes
with us. He is quite brightened up by the decision,
which was come to in a long talk under the trees at
Damien's,—D, Mrs. D, and F piping up in Chinese
with remarkable lyrical effect, and I sitting by and
enjoying the concert. Ah Fu is death on Damien; but
indeed we all exceedingly like him; he reminds us of

Colvin in many ways, which you know is a big word for us. Joe's debts are getting thinner; Tahiti is square, and genteel but languid.

The *Cormorant* is gone, to our great loss; they made us a hammock ere they left, and arranged for the relieving ship, the *Espiègle,* to make the others. Was at a school examination yesterday (girls' school) ; it is a plain-looking race; more pretty girls in the little box at Tautira than in all this big hall; but they sang, and recited, and played the piano, like any European school and for the singing (and the recitation too) far away better. Must dry up. Much love.

Ever affectionate son,
R.L.S.

21. To Lady Taylor

Lady Taylor and Sir Henry Taylor, retired Foreign Office figure, had been friends and neighbors of the Stevensons at Bournemouth.

Honolulu, June 19th, 1889

MY DEAR LADY TAYLOR,

Our new home, the *Equator,* trading schooner, rides at the buoy tonight, and we are for sea shortly. All your folk of the Roost held us for phantoms and things of the night from our first appearance; but I do wish you would try to believe in our continued existence, as flesh and blood obscurely tossed in the Pacific, or walking coral shores, and in our affection, which is more constant than becomes the breasts of such absconders. My good health does not cease to be wonderful to myself: Fanny is better in these warm places; it is the very thing for Lloyd; and in the matter of interest, the spice of life, etc., words cannot depict what fun we have. Try to have a little more patience with the fugitives, and think of us now and again among the Gilberts, where we ought to be about the time when you receive this scrap. They make no great figure on the atlas, I confess; but you will see the name there, if you look—which I wish you would, and try to conceive us as still extant. We all send the kindest remembrances to all of you; please make one of the girls write us the news to the care of R. Towns & Co., Sydney, New South Wales, where we hope to bring up about the end of the year—or later.

Do not forget yours affectionately,

ROBERT LOUIS STEVENSON

22. TO THE REVEREND DR. HYDE

One of the most searing philippics in English since the days of Alexander Pope is Stevenson's "Open Letter to the Reverend Dr. Hyde of Honolulu," attacking that Protestant minister for remarks he had made in a letter concerning Father Damien, "martyr of Molokai."

Joseph Damien de Veuster (1840–1889), born in Belgium and ordained as a Roman Catholic priest in Honolulu, spent nine years at other parishes in the Hawaiian Islands before landing on Molokai in May 1873. At Kalawao, where the Board of Health of the Kingdom had set up an isolation station for lepers, Damien labored until he died of leprosy in 1889, the year of Stevenson's first visit to Hawaii. (Leprosy is now usually referred to as

147

"Hansen's disease.") Damien has become known to the world for his ministry. One of the two statues representing the state of Hawaii in the Capitol is of Damien by Marisol (*the other is a replica of the T. R. Gould statue of Kamehameha I*).

Stevenson had admired the priest greatly for years, and spent a week at Kalawao in 1889. When he reached Samoa on December 7, he was amazed to read in a local newspaper that a proposal to erect a memorial to Damien was to be abandoned because of the publication of a defaming letter sent by Dr. C. M. Hyde of Honolulu to another minister in California. The following February, in Sydney, Australia, Stevenson obtained a copy of this letter, which had appeared in the Sydney Presbyterian. He sat down and penned this invective, which sought to destroy Hyde as much as to defend Damien.

Knowing that he risked financial ruin if Hyde should bring suits for libel, R.L.S. consulted with his family, who agreed nevertheless that it should be published. It first appeared as a pamphlet in Sydney on March 27, 1890, and thereafter was reprinted many times. Stevenson refused to take a penny in payment; as he once wrote to a London publisher, *"I do not stick at murder; I draw the line at cannibalism. I could not eat a penny roll that piece of bludgeoning brought me"* (Letters, *III, 312*). Seven months after writing it, when his anger had cooled, Stevenson called his attack *"barbarously harsh,"* and said that *"if I did it now I would defend Damien no less well, and give less pain to those who are alive. . . . On the whole, it was virtuous to defend Damien; but it was harsh to strike so hard at Dr. Hyde"* (Letters, *III, 214–215*).

The letter was reprinted in the newspaper 'Elele in Honolulu. The royalists made political capital of *it, im-*

*plying that it was the opening gun by an internationally
known adherent, attacking the missionary group who were
the strongest faction in the antiroyalist camp.*

*Residents of Hawaii have always been sensitive about
the steps taken in the past to control infection by Hansen's
disease, but visiting authors, from Stevenson to Jack London to James A. Michener, have seen the drama inherent
in the possibility of forced isolation. That Kalawao was
not always a comfortable dwelling place can be learned by
reading the little-known report to the Board of Health by
Father Damien dated March 11, 1886, reprinted in Arthur
Johnstone,* Recollections of Robert Louis Stevenson in the
Pacific (*London: Chatto & Windus, 1905*), pp. 311–327.

Sydney, February 25th, 1890

SIR,

It may probably occur to you that we have met,
and visited, and conversed; on my side, with interest.
You may remember that you have done me several
courtesies, for which I was prepared to be grateful.
But there are duties which come before gratitude,
and offenses which justly divide friends, far more,
acquaintances. Your letter to the Reverend H. B.
Gage is a document which, in my sight, if you had
filled me with bread when I was starving, if you
had sat up to nurse my father when he lay a-dying,
would yet absolve me from the bonds of gratitude.
You know enough, doubtless, of the process of canon-
ization to be aware that, a hundred years after the
death of Damien, there will appear a man charged
with the painful office of the devil's advocate. After
that noble brother of mine, and of all frail clay, shall
have lain a century at rest, one shall accuse, one de-

fend him. The circumstance is unusual that the devil's advocate should be a volunteer, should be a member of a sect immediately rival, and should make haste to take upon himself his ugly office ere the bones are cold; unusual, and of a taste which I shall leave my readers free to qualify; unusual, and to me inspiring. If I have at all learned the trade of using words to convey truth and to arouse emotion, you have at last furnished me with a subject. For it is in the interest of all mankind, and the cause of public decency in every quarter of the world, not only that Damien should be righted, but that you and your letter should be displayed at length, in their true colors, to the public eye.

To do this properly, I must begin by quoting you at large: I shall then proceed to criticize your utterance from several points of view, divine and human, in the course of which I shall attempt to draw again, and with more specification, the character of the dead saint whom it has pleased you to vilify: so much being done, I shall say farewell to you for ever.

Honolulu, August 2nd, 1889

REVEREND H. B. GAGE.

Dear Brother,—In answer to your inquiries about Father Damien, I can only reply that we who knew the man are surprised at the extravagant newspaper laudations, as if he was a most saintly philanthropist. The simple truth is, he was a coarse, dirty man, headstrong and bigoted. He was not sent to Molokai, but went there without orders; did not stay at the leper settlement (before he became one himself), but circulated freely over the whole island (less than half the island is devoted to the lepers), and he came often to Honolulu. He had no hand in the reforms and improvements inaugurated,

150

which were the work of our Board of Health, as occasion required and means were provided. He was not a pure man in his relations with women, and the leprosy of which he died should be attributed to his vices and carelessness. Others have done much for the lepers, our own ministers, the government physicians, and so forth, but never with the Catholic idea of meriting eternal life.—Yours, etc.,

C. M. HYDE.

To deal fitly with a letter so extraordinary, I must draw at the outset on my private knowledge of the signatory and his sect. It may offend others; scarcely you, who have been so busy to collect, so bold to publish, gossip on your rivals. And this is perhaps the moment when I may best explain to you the character of what you are to read: I conceive you as a man quite beyond and below the reticences of civility: with what measure you mete, with that shall it be measured you again; with you, at last, I rejoice to feel the button off the foil and to plunge home. And if in aught that I shall say I should offend others, your colleagues, whom I respect and remember with affection, I can but offer them my regret; I am not free, I am inspired by the consideration of interests far more large; and such pain as can be inflicted by anything from me must be indeed trifling when compared with the pain with which they read your letter. It is not the hangman, but the criminal, that brings dishonor on the house.

You belong, sir, to a sect—I believe my sect, and that in which my ancestors labored—which has enjoyed, and partly failed to utilize, an exceptional advantage in the islands of Hawaii. The first missionaries came; they found the land already self-purged of its old and bloody faith; they were embraced, almost on their arrival, with enthusiasm; what troubles they supported came far more from whites than from Hawaiians; and to these last they stood (in a rough figure) in the shoes of God. This is not the place to enter into the degree or causes of their failure, such as it is. One element alone is pertinent, and must here be plainly dealt with. In the course of their evangelical calling, they—or too many of them—grew rich. It may be news to you that the houses of missionaries are a cause of mocking on the streets of Honolulu. It will at least be news to you that when I returned your civil visit, the driver of my cab commented on the size, the taste, and the comfort of your home. It would have been news certainly to myself had anyone told me that afternoon that I should live to drag such matter into print. But you see, sir, how you degrade better men to your own level; and it is needful that those who are to judge betwixt you and me, betwixt Damien and the devil's advocate, should understand your letter to have been penned in a house which could raise, and that very justly, the envy and the comments of the passersby. I think (to employ a phrase of yours which I admire) it "should be attributed" to you that you have never visited the scene of Damien's life and death. If you had, and had recalled it, and looked about your pleasant rooms, even your pen perhaps would have been stayed.

Your sect (and remember, as far as any sect avows me, it is mine) has not done ill in a worldly sense in the Hawaiian Kingdom. When calamity befell their innocent parishioners, when leprosy descended and took root in the Eight Islands, a *quid pro quo* was to be looked for. To that prosperous mission, and to you, as one of its adornments, God had sent at last an opportunity. I know I am touching here upon a nerve acutely sensitive. I know that others of your colleagues look back on the inertia of your Church, and the intrusive and decisive heroism of Damien, with something almost to be called remorse. I am sure it is so with yourself; I am persuaded your letter was inspired by a certain envy, not essentially ignoble, and the one human trait to be espied in that performance. You were thinking of the lost chance, the past day; of that which should have been conceived and was not; of the service due and not rendered. *Time was,* said the voice in your ear, in your pleasant room, as you sat raging and writing; and if the words written were base beyond parallel, the rage, I am happy to repeat—it is the only compliment I shall pay you—the rage was almost virtuous. But, sir, when we have failed, and another has succeeded; when we have stood by, and another has stepped in; when we sit and grow bulky in our charming mansions, and a plain, uncouth peasant steps into the battle, under the eyes of God, and succors the afflicted, and consoles the dying, and is himself afflicted in his turn, and dies upon the field of honor—the battle cannot be retrieved as your unhappy irritation has suggested. It is a lost battle, and lost forever. One thing remained to you in your defeat—some rags of common honor; and these you have made haste to cast away.

Common honor—not the honor of having done

anything right, but the honor of not having done aught conspicuously foul; the honor of the inert: that was what remained to you. We are not all expected to be Damiens; a man may conceive his duty more narrowly, he may love his comforts better; and none will cast a stone at him for that. But will a gentleman of your reverend profession allow me an example from the fields of gallantry? When two gentlemen compete for the favor of a lady, and the one succeeds and the other is rejected, and (as will sometimes happen) matter damaging to the successful rival's credit reaches the ear of the defeated, it is held by plain men of no pretensions that his mouth is, in the circumstance, almost necessarily closed. Your Church and Damien's were in Hawaii upon a rivalry to do well: to help, to edify, to set divine examples. You having (in one huge instance) failed, and Damien succeeded, I marvel it should not have occurred to you that you were doomed to silence; that when you had been outstripped in that high rivalry, and sat inglorious in the midst of your well-being, in your pleasant room—and Damien, crowned with glories and horrors, toiled and rotted in that pigsty of his under the cliffs of Kalawao—you, the elect who would not, were the last man on earth to collect and propagate gossip on the volunteer who would and did.

I think I see you—for I try to see you in the flesh as I write these sentences—I think I see you leap at the word pigsty, a hyperbolical expression at the best. "He had no hand in the reforms," he was "a coarse, dirty man"; these were your own words; and you may think it possible that I am come to support you with fresh evidence. In a sense, it is even so. Damien has been too much depicted with a conventional halo and conventional features; so drawn by men who perhaps had not the eye to remark or the pen to express the individual; or who perhaps were only blinded and silenced by generous admiration, such as I partly envy for myself—such as you, if your soul were enlightened, would envy on your bended knees. It is the least defect of such a method of portraiture that it makes the path easy for the devil's advocate, and leaves for the misuse of the slanderer a considerable field of truth. For the truth that is suppressed by friends is the readiest weapon of the enemy. The world, in your despite, may perhaps owe you something, if your letter be the means of substituting once for all a credible likeness for a wax abstraction. For, if that world at all remember you, on the day when Damien of Molokai shall be named Saint, it will be in virtue of one work: your letter to the Reverend H. B. Gage.

You may ask on what authority I speak. It was my inclement destiny to become acquainted, not with Damien, but with Dr. Hyde. When I visited the Lazaretto, Damien was already in his resting grave. But such information as I have I gathered on the spot in conversation with those who knew him well and long: some indeed who revered his memory; but others who had sparred and wrangled with him, who beheld him with no halo, who perhaps regarded him with small respect, and through whose unprepared and scarcely partial communications the plain, human features of the man shone on me convincingly. These gave me what knowledge I possess; and I learned it in that scene where it could be most completely and sensitively understood—Kalawao, which you have never visited, about which you have never so much as endeavored to inform yourself; for, brief as your letter is, you have found the means to stumble into that confession. *"Less than one-half* of the island,"* you say, "is devoted to the lepers." Molokai— "Molokai *'āhina,"* the "gray," lofty, and most desolate island—along all its northern side plunges a front of precipice into a sea of unusual profundity. This range of cliff is, from east to west, the true end and frontier of the island. Only in one spot there projects to the ocean a certain triangular and rugged down, grassy, stony, windy, and rising in the midst into a hill with a dead crater: the whole bearing to the cliff that overhangs it somewhat the same relation as a bracket to a wall. With this hint you will now be able to pick out the leper station on a map; you will be able to judge how much of Molokai is thus cut off between the surf and precipice, whether less than a half, or less than a quarter, or a fifth, or a tenth—or, say, a twentieth; and the next time you burst into print you will be in a position to share with us the issue of your calculations.

I imagine you to be one of those persons who talk with cheerfulness of that place which oxen and wainropes could not drag you to behold. You, who do not even know its situation on the map, probably denounce sensational descriptions, stretching your limbs the while in your pleasant parlor on Beretania Street. When I was pulled ashore there one early morning, there sat with me in the boat two sisters, bidding farewell (in humble imitation of Damien) to the lights and joys of human life. One of these wept silently; I could not withhold myself from joining her. Had you been there, it is my belief that nature would have triumphed even in you; and as the boat drew but a little nearer, and you beheld the stairs crowded with abominable deformations of our common manhood, and saw yourself landing in the midst of such a population as only now and then surrounds us in the horror of a nightmare—what a haggard eye you would have rolled over your reluctant shoulder toward the house on Beretania Street! Had you gone on; had you found every fourth face a blot upon the landscape; had you visited the hospital and seen the butt ends of human beings lying there almost unrecognizable, but still breathing, still thinking, still remembering; you would have understood that life in the Lazaretto is an ordeal from which the nerves of a man's spirit shrink, even as his eye quails under the brightness of the sun; you would have felt it was (even today) a pitiful place to visit and a hell to dwell in. It is not the fear of possible infection. That seems a little thing when compared with the pain, the pity, and the disgust of the visitor's surroundings, and the atmosphere of affliction, disease, and physical disgrace in which he breathes. I do not think I am a man more than usually timid; but I never recall the days and nights I spent upon that island promontory (eight days and seven nights), without heartfelt thankfulness that I am somewhere else. I find in my diary that I speak of my stay as a "grinding experience." I have once jotted in the margin, "*harrowing* is the word," and when the *Mokoli'i* bore me at last toward the outer world, I kept repeating to myself, with a new conception of their pregnancy, those simple words of the song: " 'Tis the most distressful country that ever yet was seen."

And observe: that which I saw and suffered from was a settlement purged, bettered, beautified; the new village built, the hospital and the Bishop Home excellently arranged; the sisters, the doctor, and the missionaries, all indefatigable in their noble tasks. It was a different place when Damien came there and made his great renunciation, and slept that first night under a tree amidst his rotting brethren, alone with pestilence and looking forward (with what courage, with what pitiful sinkings of dread, God only knows) to a lifetime of dressing sores and stumps.

You will say, perhaps, I am too sensitive, that sights as painful abound in cancer hospitals and are confronted daily by doctors and nurses. I have long learned to admire and envy the doctors and the nurses. But there is no cancer hospital so large and populous as Kalawao and Kalaupapa, and in such a matter every fresh case, like every inch of length in the pipe of an organ, deepens the note of the impression; for what daunts the onlooker is that monstrous sum of human suffering by which he stands surrounded. Lastly, no doctor or nurse is called upon to enter once for all the doors of that Gehenna; they do not say farewell, they need not abandon hope on its sad threshold; they but go for a time to their high calling, and can look forward as they go to relief, to recreation, and to rest. But Damien shut to with his own hand the doors of his own sepulcher.

I shall now extract three passages from my diary at Kalawao.

LETTERS FROM HAWAII

Damien is dead and already somewhat ungratefully remembered in the field of his labors and sufferings. "He was a good man, but very officious," says one. Another tells me he had fallen (as other priests so easily do) into something of the ways and habits of thought of a kanaka; but he had the wit to recognize the fact, and the good sense to laugh at [over] it. A plain man it seems he was; I cannot find he was a popular.

After Ragsdale's death [Ragsdale was a famous luna, or overseer, of the unruly settlement] there followed a brief term of office by Father Damien which served only to publish the weakness of that noble man. He was rough in his ways, and he had no control. Authority was relaxed; Damien's life was threatened, and he was soon eager to resign.

Of Damien I begin to have an idea. He seems to have been a man of the peasant class, certainly of the peasant type: shrewd, ignorant and bigoted, yet with an open mind, and capable of receiving and digesting a reproof if it were bluntly administered; superbly generous in the least thing as well as in the greatest, and as ready to give his last shirt (although not without human grumbling) as he had been to sacrifice his life; essentially indiscreet and officious, which made him a troublesome colleague; domineering in all his ways, which made him incurably unpopular with the kanakas, but yet destitute of real authority, so that his boys laughed at him and he must carry out his wishes by the means of bribes. He learned to have a mania for doctoring; and set up the kanakas against the remedies of his regular rivals: perhaps (if anything matter at all in the treatment of such a disease) the worst thing that he did, and certainly the easiest. The best and worst of the man appear very plainly in his dealings with Mr. Chapman's money; he had originally laid it out [intended to lay it out] entirely for the benefit of Catholics, and even so not wisely; but after a long, plain talk, he admitted his error fully and revised the list. The sad state of the boys' home is in part the result of his lack of control; in part, of his own slovenly ways and false ideas of hygiene. Brother officials used to call it Damien's Chinatown. "Well," they would say, "your Chinatown keeps growing." And he would laugh with perfect good nature, and adhere to his errors with perfect obstinacy. So much I have gathered of truth about this plain, noble human brother and father of ours; his imperfections are the traits of his face, by which we know him for our fellow; his martyrdom and his example nothing can lessen or annul; and only a person here on the spot can properly appreciate their greatness.

I have set down these private passages, as you perceive, without correction; thanks to you, the public has them in their bluntness. They are almost a list of the man's faults, for it is rather these that I was seeking: with his virtues, with the heroic profile of his life, I and the world were already sufficiently acquainted. I was besides a little suspicious of Catholic testimony; in no ill sense, but merely because Damien's admirers and disciples were the least likely to be critical. I know you will be more suspicious still; and the facts set down above were one and all collected from the lips of Protestants who had opposed the father in his life. Yet I am strangely deceived, or they build up the image of a man, with all his weaknesses, essentially heroic, and alive with rugged honesty, generosity, and mirth.

Take it for what it is, rough private jottings of the worst sides of Damien's character, collected from the lips of those who had labored with and (in your own phrase) "knew the man"—though I question whether Damien would have said that he knew you.

Take it, and observe with wonder how well you were served by your gossips, how ill by your intelligence and sympathy; in how many points of fact we are at one, and how widely our appreciations vary. There is something wrong here—either with you or me. It is possible, for instance, that you, who seem to have so many ears in Kalawao, had heard of the affair of Mr. Chapman's money and were singly struck by Damien's intended wrongdoing. I was struck with that also, and set it fairly down; but I was struck much more by the fact that he had the honesty of mind to be convinced. I may here tell you that it was a long business; that one of his colleagues sat with him late into the night, multiplying arguments and accusations; that the father listened as usual with "perfect good nature and perfect obstinacy"; but at the last, when he was persuaded—"Yes," said he, "I am very much obliged to you; you have done me a service; it would have been a theft." There are many (not Catholics merely) who require their heroes and saints to be infallible; to these the story will be painful; not to the true lovers, patrons, and servants of mankind.

And I take it, this is a type of our division—that you are one of those who have an eye for faults and failures, that you take a pleasure to find and publish them, and that, having found them, you make haste to forget the overvailing virtues and the real success which had alone introduced them to your knowledge. It is a dangerous frame of mind. That you may understand how dangerous, and into what a situation it has already brought you, we will (if you please) go hand in hand through the different phrases of your letter, and candidly examine each from the point of view of its truth, its appositeness, and its charity.

Damien was coarse.

It is very possible. You make us sorry for the lepers, who had only a coarse old peasant for their friend and father. But you, who were so refined, why were you not there, to cheer them with the lights of culture? Or may I remind you that we have some reason to doubt if John the Baptist were genteel; and in the case of Peter, on whose career you doubtless dwell approvingly in the pulpit, no doubt at all he was a "coarse, headstrong" fisherman! Yet even in our Protestant Bibles, Peter is called Saint.

Damien was dirty.

He was. Think of the poor lepers annoyed with this dirty comrade! But the clean Dr. Hyde was at his food in a fine house.

Damien was headstrong.

I believe you are right again; and I thank God for his strong head and heart.

Damien was bigoted.

I am not fond of bigots myself, because they are not fond of me. But what is meant by bigotry, that we should regard it as a blemish in a priest? Damien believed his own religion with the simplicity of a peasant or a child; as I would I could suppose that you do. For this, I wonder at him some way off; and had that been his only character, should have avoided him in life. But the point of interest in Damien, which has caused him to be so much talked about and made him at last the subject of your pen and mine, was that, in him, his bigotry, his intense and narrow faith, wrought potently for good, and strengthened him to be one of the world's heroes and exemplars.

Damien was not sent to Molokai, but went there without orders.

Is this a misreading? Or do you really mean the words for blame? I have heard Christ, in the pulpits of our Church, held up for imitation on the ground that His sacrifice was voluntary. Does Dr. Hyde think otherwise?

Damien did not stay at the settlement, etc.

It is true he was allowed many indulgences. Am I to understand that you blame the father for profiting by these, or the officers for granting them? In either case, it is a mighty Spartan standard to issue from the house on Beretania Street; and I am convinced you will find yourself with few supporters.

Damien had no hand in the reforms, etc.

I think even you will admit that I have already been frank in my description of the man I am defending; but before I take you up upon this head, I will be franker still, and tell you that perhaps nowhere in the world can a man taste a more pleasurable sense of contrast than when he passes from Damien's "Chinatown" at Kalawao to the beautiful Bishop Home at Kalaupapa. At this point, in my desire to make all fair for you, I will break my rule and adduce Catholic testimony. Here is a passage from my diary about my visit to the Chinatown, from which you will see how it is (even now) regarded by its own officials:

We went round all the dormitories, refectories, etc.— dark and dingy enough, with a superficial cleanliness, which he [Mr. Dutton, the lay-brother] did not seek to defend. "It is almost decent," said he; "the sisters will make that all right when we get them here."

And yet I gathered it was already better since Damien was dead, and far better than when he was there alone and had his own (not always excellent) way. I have now come far enough to meet you on a common ground of fact; and I tell you that, to a mind not prejudiced by jealousy, all the reforms of the Lazaretto, and even those which he most vigorously opposed, are properly the work of Damien. They are the evidence of his success; they are what his heroism provoked from the reluctant and the careless. Many were before him in the field; Mr. Meyer, for instance, of whose faithful work we hear too little: there have been many since; and some had more worldly wisdom, though none had more devotion, than our saint. Before his day, even you will confess, they had effected little. It was his part, by one striking act of martyrdom, to direct all men's eyes on that distressful country. At a blow, and with the price of his life, he made the place illustrious and public. And that, if you will consider largely, was the one reform needful, pregnant of all that should succeed. It brought money; it brought (best individual addition of them all) the sisters; it brought supervision, for public opinion and public interest landed with the man at Kalawao. If ever any man brought reforms, and died to bring them, it was he. There is not a clean cup or towel in the Bishop Home but dirty Damien washed it.

Damien was not a pure man in his relations with women, etc.

How do you know that? Is this the nature of the

conversation in that house on Beretania Street which the cabman envied, driving past?—racy details of the misconduct of the poor peasant priest, toiling under the cliffs of Molokai?

Many have visited the station before me; they seem not to have heard the rumor. When I was there I heard many shocking tales, for my informants were men speaking with the plainness of the laity; and I heard plenty of complaints of Damien. Why was this never mentioned? And how came it to you in the retirement of your clerical parlor?

But I must not even seem to deceive you. This scandal, when I read it in your letter, was not new to me. I had heard it once before; and I must tell you how. There came to Samoa a man from Honolulu; he, in a public house on the beach, volunteered the statement that Damien had "contracted the disease from having connection with the female lepers"; and I find a joy in telling you how the report was welcomed in a public house. A man sprang to his feet; I am not at liberty to give his name, but from what I heard I doubt if you would care to have him to dinner in Beretania Street. "You miserable little ———" (here is a word I dare not print, it would so shock your ears). "You miserable little ———," he cried, "if the story were a thousand times true, can't you see you are a million times a lower ——— for daring to repeat it?" I wish it could be told of you that when the report reached you in your house, perhaps after family worship, you had found in your soul enough holy anger to receive it with the same expressions; ay, even with that one which I dare not print; it would not need to have been blotted away, like Uncle Toby's oath, by the tears of the recording angel; it would have been counted to you for your brightest righteousness. But you have deliberately chosen the part of the man from Honolulu, and you have played it with improvements of your own. The man from Honolulu—miserable, leering creature—communicated the tale to a rude knot of beachcombing drinkers in a public house, where (I will so far agree with your temperance opinions) man is not always at his noblest; and the man from Honolulu had himself been drinking—drinking, we may charitably fancy, to excess. It was to your "Dear Brother, the Reverend H. B. Gage," that you chose to communicate the sickening story; and the blue ribbon which adorns your portly bosom forbids me to allow you the extenuating plea that you were drunk when it was done. Your "dear brother"—a brother indeed —made haste to deliver up your letter (as a means of grace, perhaps) to the religious papers; where, after many months, I found and read and wondered at it, and whence I have now reproduced it for the wonder of others. And you and your dear brother have, by this cycle of operations, built up a contrast very edifying to examine in detail. The man whom you would not care to have to dinner, on the one side; on the other, the Reverend Dr. Hyde and the Reverend H. B. Gage: the Apia barroom, the Honolulu manse.

But I fear you scarce appreciate how you appear to your fellow men; and to bring it home to you, I will suppose your story to be true. I will suppose— and God forgive me for supposing it—that Damien faltered and stumbled in his narrow path of duty; I will suppose that, in the horror of his isolation, perhaps in the fever of incipient disease, he, who was doing so much more than he had sworn, failed in the letter of his priestly oath—he, who was so much a better man than either you or me, who did what we have never dreamed of daring—he too tasted of our common frailty. "O, Iago, the pity of it!" The least tender should be moved to tears; the most incredulous to prayer. And all that you could do was to pen your letter to the Reverend H. B. Gage!

Is it growing at all clear to you what a picture you have drawn of your own heart? I will try yet once again to make it clearer. You had a father: suppose this tale were about him, and some informant brought it to you, proof in hand—I am not making too high an estimate of your emotional nature when I suppose you would regret the circumstance? That you would feel the tale of frailty the more keenly since it shamed the author of your days? And that the last thing you would do would be to publish it in the religious press? Well, the man who tried to do what Damien did is my father, and the father of the man in the Apia bar, and the father of all who love goodness; and he was your father too, if God had given you grace to see it.

ROBERT LOUIS STEVENSON

23. TO THE EDITOR OF THE *Advertiser*

Not long after Stevenson fell ill at Sans Souci in October 1893, he became annoyed by a newspaper account stating that the management of the hotel had been charged with keeping a "disorderly house"—presumably in viola tion of liquor-control ordinances. He responded to a standing invitation by Arthur Johnstone, editor of the Advertiser, *by sending the letter below. It did not appear in the newspaper but was printed first in 1905 in Johnstone's* Recollections *(pp. 108–109, and in facsimile after p. 200). Stevenson's dislike for disorderly telephones is amusingly revealed.*

Waikiki, Honolulu, H. I., 6th October 1893

SIR,

Will you allow a harmless sick man, who has just made out eight days of sickness here, to express his amazement and his wholesale disapproval at the nickname recently tacked upon it in the papers: A Disorderly House? My bedroom is now in the heart of the establishment, opening upon all the public rooms. No one can arrive, no one can depart, by day or night, but I must hear them. I have had a high fever: you will regard it as an obvious rider that I was in a state to be easily annoyed. Will you believe it, sir, the only annoyance that has befallen me in this Disorderly Establishment was two nights ago, when the telephone broke out bleating like a deserted infant from the nigh dining room; I dare never, from a variety of prudential considerations, approach this interesting instrument myself; I had no choice but to summon others who should prove more bold; and for a considerable interval in the gaunt midnight, the telephone bell and I performed a duet. At length Mr. Simpson came to the rescue, fearlessly tackled the apparatus, and learned that the *Adams* was demanding her chief engineer.

If this be disorder—well, I will agree. The introduction of the telephone into our bed and board, into

our business and bosoms, partakes of the nature of intrusion. But one house in Honolulu is not more private than another. And to me, who pass my days
listening to the wind and the waves along the reef,
I can but say that I desire to find no quieter haven
than the *Sans Souci*; and may well add, with the
poet, "In a more sacred or sequestered bower, nor
nymph nor Faunus haunted."

I am, Sir, your obedient servant,
ROBERT LOUIS STEVENSON

24. TO THE DEAR EDITOR
[OF THE Advertiser]

*This personal note to Johnstone was not published until
it appeared in the editor's* Recollections, *p. 120. Because
of Stevenson's illness, a second talk before the Honolulu
Scottish Thistle Club had to be canceled.*

Sans Souci, October 20th, 1893

SIR,

Will you please to state—*this note is not for the
public*—that, owing to an interference of Providence,
abetted by my French doctor, the talk announced to
take place tomorrow afternoon must be indefinitely
postponed. I do not believe the effort would seriously
hurt my health, and, as you know, I would rather
take a wee risk than to disappoint so many of my
friends in Honolulu; but Dr. Trousseau and Mrs.
Stevenson are insistent, and I must yield. Perhaps
they are right, but I hope not; for it would be hard
to believe so, just when I am learning to forget I am
an invalid. The fever has entirely left me, and I am
certainly convalescent. We hope to be able to return

by the steamer due about October 27, in which case there is a small kindness I shall ask you to do for me —collecting a fact or two to be forwarded at your pleasure to Apia.—I am, sir, in haste,

R.L.S.

25. To W. F. Reynolds

Taalolo, Stevenson's young servant, had suffered from the measles and then had attended his ill master, so that he had seen little of Honolulu. Thoughtfully, near the time of departure, R.L.S. here asks an acquaintance to arrange a sightseeing tour for the boy. This note first appeared in Johnstone, p. 276.

Sans Souci, Waikiki

DEAR SIR,

As I am still abominably out of sorts, I have taken the desperate step of chucking my Samoan cookboy (he is the bearer) at the head of total strangers! Can you find nobody who would be a guide to him? A boy of ten or so would suit best; and I want him to see Punchbowl, and the railway, and Pearl Lochs, and all the Raree Show. I am perfectly willing to pay for him in reason.

If you cannot help him to this, somebody that would take him out and bring him back sober; well, talk a little to him an you love me!—and talk slow.

Yours truly,

ROBERT LOUIS STEVENSON

III

POEMS FROM
HAWAII

POEMS FROM HAWAII

*The six poems by Stevenson written during his so-
journ in Hawaii in 1889 are neither among his best
nor his poorest verses. Most of them were quickly
composed to celebrate certain occasions. At least one
of them—"To Princess Ka'iulani"—will be quoted
so long as the people of Hawaii remember their ill-
fated heiress-apparent, Ka'iulani. The poems are
numbered for convenience in reference.*

1. To King Kalākaua

This unusual sonnet (rhyming in couplets) was presented to King Kalākaua during the Waikiki luau on February 3, along with a mounted golden pearl obtained on the "silver ship"—the Casco—*in the Tuamotu Islands. The source is Stevenson,* Collected Works, *Thistle edition* (*New York: Charles Scribner's Sons, XVI,* Ballads and Other Poems), *p. 234.*

The Silver Ship, my King—that was her name
In the bright islands whence your fathers came—
The Silver Ship, at rest from winds and tides,
Below your palace in your harbor rides:
And the seafarers, sitting safe on shore,
Like eager merchants count their treasures o'er.
One gift they find, one strange and lovely thing,
Now doubly precious since it pleased a king.

The right, my liege, is ancient as the lyre
For bards to give to kings what kings admire.
'Tis mine to offer for Apollo's sake;
And since the gift is fitting, yours to take.
To golden hands the golden pearl I bring:
The ocean jewel to the island king.

2. To Mrs. Caroline Bush

To celebrate the fifty-third birthday of Mrs. Bush, the Stevensons presented her with a length of soft silk from which to make a holoku. After a stroll on the beach, R.L.S. composed for the presentation these verses, which the lady long cherished. The source is Arthur Johnstone, Recollections of Robert Louis Stevenson in the Pacific (*London: Chatto & Windus, 1905*), *pp. 305–306.*

Dear Lady, tapping at your door,
    Some little verses stand,
And beg on this auspicious day
    To come and kiss your hand.

Their syllables all counted right,
    Their rhymes each in its place,
Like birthday children, at the door
    They wait to see your face.

Rise, lady, rise and let them in.
    Fresh from the fairy shore,
They bring you things you wish to have,
    Each in its pinafore.

For they have been to Wishing Land
    This morning in the dew,
All, all your dearest wishes bring—
    All granted—home to you.

What these may be they would not tell,
    And could not if they would;
They take the packets sealed to you,
    As trusty servants should.

But there was one that looked like love,
    And one that smelt like health,
And one that had a jingling sound
    I fancy might be wealth.

Ah, well, they are but wishes still;
    But lady dear, for you
I know that all you wish is kind.
    I pray it all come true.

POEMS FROM HAWAII

3. To Princess Ka'iulani

When Princess Ka'iulani, teenage daughter of A. S. Cleghorn, seemed loath to leave her islands for schooling in Great Britain, Stevenson tried to tell her how she would make new friends and bring brightness there. He then inscribed the following lines in her red plush autograph album. The source is Ballads and Other Poems, *p. 235.*

> Forth from her land to mine she goes,
> The island maid, the island rose,
> Light of heart and bright of face:
> The daughter of a double race.
> Her islands here, in Southern sun,
> Shall mourn their Ka'iulani gone,
> And I, in her dear banyan shade,
> Look vainly for my little maid.
>
> But our Scots islands far away
> Shall glitter with unwonted day,
> And cast for once their tempests by
> To smile in Ka'iulani's eye.

Written in April to Ka'iulani in the April of her age; and at Waikiki, within easy walk of Ka'iulani's banyan! When she comes to my land and her father's, and the rain beats upon the window (as I fear it will), let her look at this page; it will be like a weed gathered and pressed at home; and she will remember her own islands, and the shadow of the mighty tree; and she will hear the peacocks screaming in the dusk and the wind blowing in the palms; and she will think of her father sitting there alone.—R.L.S.

4. To Mother Marianne

This poem, presented to the mother superior of the Bishop Home at the Kalawao settlement, expresses Stevenson's delight in the devotion of the Catholic sisters at their tasks among the lepers. The verses are dated May 22, the day of Stevenson's arrival and probably before he had conversed with Mother Marianne at the Home. In a rush of admiration he must have penned the lines that later were dedicated to the head of the Home where he visited. The source is Sister Martha Mary McGaw, Stevenson in Hawaii *(Honolulu: University of Hawaii Press, 1950), p. 98.*

To see the infinite pity of this place,
The mangled limb, the devastated face,
The innocent sufferers smiling at the rod,
A fool were tempted to deny his God.

He sees, and shrinks; but if he look again,
Lo, beauty springing from the breast of pain!—
He marks the sisters on the painful shores,
And even a fool is silent and adores.

Kalawao, May 22nd, 1889.

5. The High Winds of Nuuanu

At the urgent request of Arthur Johnstone, editor of the Pacific Commercial Advertiser, *for a poem about Honolulu for his newspaper, R.L.S. wrote the following description in blank verse, depicting the valley leading to a famed precipice behind the city. The author intended to add a few more lines but did nothing thereafter on the subject, and the poem was salvaged and first published in Johnstone's book, pages 307–308.*

Within the famous valley of that name,
Now twice or thrice the high wind blows each year,
Until you hear it pulsing through the gorge
In spiteful gusts: sometimes it comes with bursts
Of rain, in fiercer squalls; and, howling down the glen,
It breaks great tropic fronds like stems of clay.
Lo! then, the unbending palms and rugged dates,
Loud-whistling, strain in each recurrent blast,
Like things alive!—or fall, with roots uptorn,
The feathered algarobas, as the gale
Treads out its wasteful pathway to the sea!
Thus twice or thrice Nuuanu's high winds rage,
Threshing the vale till quakes the Island's heart!
Ten other months are filled with nerveless rest,
Mid cooling breezes and down-dropping showers;
At night the dark-blue vault arching the vale,
Studded with stars innumerable and bright!
While fleecy clouds outdrifting to the sea,
Make shadows in the moonlight on the sward.
Here dwell the Islanders in peace, until
The blasts again sweep down from Northern seas.

6. From Number Two to Anita Neumann

Visiting the Sans Souci home of the Honorable Paul Neumann one day, Stevenson found the seventeen-year-old daughter perusing a poem from an anonymous admirer. Amused, R.L.S. composed these verses for her that afternoon, referring to the unknown versifier as "Number One" and to himself as "Number Two." The Stevenson poem hinges upon a single rhyme. The source is Johnstone, pp. 306–307.

I see where you are driving, dear,
    And haste to meet your views.
The nameless man was Number One—
    And here is Number Two's.

TRAVELS IN HAWAII

What special charm shall I select
    To honor in the Muse?
Your mind—your heart, Anita! dyed
    In early morning blues,
With just a hint of fire to warm
    Its cold amoral hues?
Your grey eyes, or your slender hands?
    In faith I may not choose!

An angel inexpert, untried,
    Lingering as angel's use—
Too nice to wet your perfect feet
    In merely earthly dews.
The day shall come—it is not far—
    When life shall claim its dues,
And fair Anita to fair love
    Her hand no more refuse.

Alas! the rhyme is nearly out
    I was so rash to choose!
Anita, with my right goodwill,
    Take this of Number Two's.

R.L.S.

APPENDIX

JOURNAL OF A VISIT
TO THE KONA COAST

*Stevenson's Journal of his visit to the Kona Coast,
here printed for the first time through the courtesy
of the Henry E. Huntington Library at San Marino,
California, is a fascinating document. Written daily
on the spot, the scrawled nineteen pages require much
effort to decipher. They are here transcribed verbatim (including obvious errors). The Journal contains much description and comment that was omitted, perhaps wisely, from the final sketches based on
it. Hardly a line of the Journal was published un-
changed. First impressions were often canceled; on
the other hand, a line in the Journal was sometimes
expanded to a powerful passage. The account of the
trial at Ho'okena is lengthy, perhaps because Stevenson, trained as a lawyer in Scotland, fancied his ex-
pertise as a friend of the court. R.L.S. must have
been reading about this time* A Residence of Twenty-
One Years in the Sandwich Islands (*1847*) *by the
Reverend Hiram Bingham, one of the first company
of missionaries to land in the islands in* 1820; *most*

of the marginal quotations from "Binamu" [Bing-ham] concerning nakedness and heathenism were excised in the final draft. A student could learn much from comparing the Journal with the printed chapters and noting Stevenson's revisions and omissions, and might do worse than imitate his self-editing, as Stevenson himself played the "sedulous ape" to a score of other writers while hammering out his own personal style.

KONA COAST HAWAII

Saturday. Whaleboat full of barrels and passengers and ourselves, somewhat intermingled put off from the steamer in the rain. Hookena was visible under a low black cliff, streaked with white lichen— flat, black walls, making a foreshore, with the surf lazily turning and making fountains at their edge, itself a little grove of shabby palms and tropical fruit trees, a white church, and some score of neat, white, verandahed and trelliced dwelling houses. At the landing place thirty or forty score men and women stood in the rain, and all along the black rocks of the foreshore horses, donkeys and mules.

We foreigners were helped out upon a point of reef, where the next wave submerged us to the knees. There we all stood however, the rain drenching us from above the sea from below, like folk mesmerised; and like folk mesmerised, the crowd from the beach looked back at us. At last I set off wading ashore; and the purser introduced me to my host, an old gentleman with a hatband of peacock feather, a face like an old trusty dog's, no eyes, and no English: "House by'm by," said he, and resting on his laurels led me without further speech through the crowd to a large open shed. A table heaped with goods divided it across; so that I knew it was the store. On three sides it was open; you mounted to it by some five or six steps of wooden stair; and the house which filled the fourth side was reached by ten steps more. Perhaps 20 men women and children stood on the shop level; and half a dozen more occupied the veranda of the house. Only one old woman paid the least attention to the haole [white person]; but she hailed Mr Nahinu with some question, in the answer to which I heard the king's name taken not I hope in vain. I put in the time, and consoled myself, flirting with a little maid of seven; I am aware I made a deep impression in this virgin heart, for she has turned up looking for me since. One woman in the shed was like Mrs Air; one of the rowers coming in was like a Marquesan, whose name escapes me; and these resemblances made me homesick. Presently the mail was delivered. A great packet of *Ka Nupepa 'Elele* among the rest; and I saw one capible middle-aged man tear that open, turn straight to the story page, read through the current number of one of the serials and then drop the paper like the rind of a sucked orange.

At last off to Nahinu's. Portraits of Kalakaua, Kamehameha 3rd, Lunalilo, the present queen, and Queen Victoria. Silence. Walk out at night. Seaside resort effect very strong; the black rock and the black drystone dykes like peat.

Sunday. Walk above the cliff, call on the Roberts [Mr. and Mrs. Robert Amalu], discuss the new way of teaching.

APPENDIX

Monday. 5½ hours in the saddle. At first over the black basalt, bushes and creepers here and there, looking very green after the rain in this black setting: black drystone dykes enclosing further wastes; here and there, prickly pears growing like standard trees and giving the only shade: under one 3 cows under another a cuddy [donkey]. The trees begin to heave up and presently we come to a house in an orchard of n's [papayas] with their semi palmlike growth, and collar of green gourds. An outhouse contains the great water barrel from which we drink: on all the Kona coast no water but rain water stand in barrels or cisterns, but very sweet and palatable: the house belongs to Mr. Nahinu, but an American lives in it who tries to make butter and (if I gather rightly) cannot. 3 rms. I look at them through the windows: in the first milk pans and the remainder of the butterman's breakfast; in the second a bed; in the third, a very few clothes hanging from pegs, and on the floor, two seaside library novels: one is backside up and I cannot tell what it is, the name of the other I make out: "Little Loo." Happy Mr Clark Russel, making life sweet to this exile, in his orchard of n's, high above the surf, in the forest edge, where the wind comes so freshly. Beyond we plunge into the forest. It grows at first very sparse and park-like, with only moderate timber; the trees of a pale verdure but healthy, and the parasytes (per contra) mostly dead. As we advance, nature changes; the ground is still a wilderness of rock and stone and boulder, but soil occupies the interstices, we pass through almost continuous coffee bushes, thick with green berries, a sedgelike grass covers the ground and the horses munch it as they go. Candlenut kukui trees with their white foliage made isles; breadfruit trees are peppered over all, but never any well to do, or so it strikes a beholder from the south: there are fine mangos, one side of them stained a purplish red sometimes, which gives the autumnal note never absent in tropical forests. The same effect is produced by a certain aerial creeper, which drops, you might suppose from heaven like the wreck of an old kite, and hangs in treetops with a pendant raffle of air roots, the whole of an autumnal brown, comparable to wintry beaches. They are clannish plants; five or six may be planted in a single tree; thirty or forty on a single grove; the wood dies under them to a skeleton; and they swing there like things hung out to wash, over the death they have provoked. A bird or two whistled sweetly. In this early part we are continually in view of the whole falling seaboard, the white edge of surf now soundless, the high blue sea marked by tide rips, and showing under the clouds of an opalescent milky white. Here, too, I observed a spider planting its abhorred St Andrews Cross right against sea and sky, five feet from either treetop, so wide was its death gossamer spread, so huge was the ugly beast itself. Next the wood closed about us very deep and close, ferns joined their fronds above a horseman's head, great dead trees soared high into the air and were clothed three parts of their height with a creeperlike pandanus; it was very hot, the air reached us faintly; we stopped and collected gum from a tree which we all ate thenceforth; stopped again because my girth had broken; came to Mr Roberts coffee plantation—he and nineteen other natives have

bought a great tract of land here—60,000 acres, for
4,000 dollars; and his coffee is now planted; he has
a chinaman to mind it, Hawaiians will not work—
came at last out of the wood, with a nobler view than
ever, a catholic church, and a good many houses,
some of grass in the old style, others spick and span
with outside stair, and balcony, and trellice, and
white paint and green, according to the local fashion.
One house all white, with double balcony, and of
imposing presence—I counted 15 windows—attracted my attention. "This is a fine house," said I.
"Outside," said Mr. Robert smiling. "That is the
way with natives; they spend money on the outside."
And doubtless this proprietor is happy, for Nahinu
[Amalu], in giving his wife an itinerary after we
returned, referred to it as "Ka hale nui" [the big
house]. We stopped here, sat in the verandah and
had a drink of water. Sure enough in the lower room
where I went there was not one stick of furniture;
only mats on the floor and on the wall photographs of
the (inevitable) royal family, and two lithographs.
One I knew at first sight was Garfield; the other
tempted and tantalised me—it could not be—and yet
it must, I thought; and it was indeed this dubiety that
carried me over the threshold; and sure enough it
was the Duke of Thunder; his name printed under
his effigies in the Hawaiianised form of Nelesona.
I thought this a fine instance of fame that his face and
empty sleeve should be drawn on stone in San Francisco, and lettered for a market in the eight islands.
And then I had a cold fit, and wondered if after all
these good folk knew anything of his world-shaking
deeds and gunpowder weaknesses; and turning to

Mr Robert, I asked of him the question. Yes: it appeared, the Hawaiians knew of Nelesona; there had been a story translated in the newspapers, where he figured. Well, this too was fame. In the verandah, there was much talk of my voyages, and what particularly pleases everyone, of my sight of Kauwealoha in the fabled land, Kahiki [actually this Hawaiian missionary served in the Marquesas, not Tahiti].

We returned by a lower road over the black open, crossing for a great while, a strange waste of lava, ravines, spires, well holes showing the entrance of vast subterranean vaults in whose profundities our horse hooves doubtless echoed; the whole covered with stone fiarituri, sometimes like a rude kind sort of coral, sometimes more fantastically carved, like debris from the workshop of a brutal sculptor—dogs heads, devils, stone trees—from a distance it looked like a scorched growth of heather, so intricate was the random workmanship; plants found a frequent root, mountain (not mummy) apples, growing twenty feet high. Through all this the break neck path wound and descended, drawing ever nearer to the sea; and at last when we were already close down, a cliff hove up suddenly on the landward hand, very rugged and broken, streaked with lichen, laddered with gree lianas and pierced with the apertures of half a hundred caves. Two of these were piously sealed with doors of recent erection: they were sepulchral catacombs of ancient alii [nobility] and kahunas [priests].

Now at last the rain was threatening, and we put our horses to the gallop, and clattered home, as it humbly appeared to me upon the verge of eternity.

Tuesday May 1st [April 30]. A crowd about the court house. I went along and found a fine wooden room with a couple of tables then a few chairs and a bench along one wall. The judge a very intelligent, serious native sat at one of the tables taking his notes; two policemen, with their bright metal badges represented force, standing at attention or bustling forth upon errands; the plaintiff, a blue-eyed portuguese, speedily hired Nahinu to represent his interests, at a fee I subsequently learned of two dollars, and that sum not exorbitant, since any native may, and any chinaman does, earn a dollar a day picking cotton. I was myself accommodated with a chair by the express desire of the Bench and found myself ere long engaged in the interpretation of a statute. It was a pretty point; and as usual with pretty points there was nothing in it. The portuguese had for some years past kept a store and some cattle; all had been well with the natives, his store stood always open, it was standing open seven miles away at that very hour; and when his cattle strayed, they were duly impounded and he paid his quarter dollar. But recently there had come a change; a gentleman of great acuteness and a thousand imperfect talents married into the family of a neighboring proprietor; and all of a sudden the Portugee's cattle were kept back and starved, the fine rose somehow or other to half a dollar a head, and lastly one cow disappeared. The Portuguese had no doubt the newcomer was at the bottom of the change; he brought his case against the proprietor; and behold, it was the newcomer who appeared to defend. I saw him there, seated at his ease, spectacles on forehead, the left hand of the bench: very much of a gentleman in looks, dressed in faultless European clothes; and presently I had a real good fortune—I saw him rise to speak. It appears he has already stood for parliament and means to stand again; and I know not where you could find a constituency at home to refuse him, though here where he was known, he had been defeated. "The people do not think him honest," I was told. Honesty, to my European eyes seems nothing in a candidate: and here was an amateur (or a comedian if you prefer) of the first order of merit. I understood not above half a dozen words, but I heard him with entire pleasure, followed each fresh position, knew when he was enumerating points in his own favor, and he was enumerating them against him, when he drew a conclusion, when he put a question per absurdum, when (after a due pause) he smilingly replied to it. The judge heard him out, Nahinu answered, the native statutes were consulted, and then the English, and here it was that I appeared upon the scene like Daniel. The people did not think him honest, some judge (on a particular occasion) had inclined to the same view, and this talented gentleman was disbarred. But he claimed, under a clause of the statute, to appear for "his own family." It went against him; he accepted his defeat in splendid style, hired a very dull lawyer, and the interest of the case determined. The Portuguese won. I felt he would when his adversary had thus lost his Queen at the first move; and late in the afternoon, the capable judge rode off again with his portfolio under his arm. No court could have been more equally and decently conducted; judge, parties, lawyers, police and by-standers all at their best; and but for the Portuguese, the business was entirely native.

The court was still sitting when I rode off with Mr Robert—the schoolmaster going before on a trumpeting black stallion, myself following on a mare of visibly amorous complexion, with black care upon the cantle—past the courthouse, past the church, past the little low wooden house on the lawn, which had taken my eye in the first sight, and which I now found was a house of detention for lepers. Two were there now, waiting till a schooner had discharged house boards further up the coast, and should call here to carry them to Molokai. One of them, I gathered, had been captured after a desperate resistance. Another had recently escaped. His wife it was supposed had brought him a knife; he had threatened a poor woman (his only fellow prisoner) into silence, had cut a small hole in the floor, squeezed himself through and fled to the mountains, where he was now at large. I had heard of two such ghastly maroons in Oahu: how many others await death and abide the mountain rains who can tell?

Our way led us along the lava-district of the coast. This is a contorted crust formed in cooling, and which every here and there breaks down (as I have said) in a sort of well-hole, and shows the mouths of branching galleries. The whole coast is similarly undermined. The sea may be heard raving below inland houses; there is one practicable gauge of miles, which was sometimes used in war in the old days; and hence it comes that the face of every cliff is darkened with the mouths of caverns. A little grass and

some flowering bushes spring in the fissures of the
lava; donkeys and cattle are everywhere; everywhere
too their whitened bones, telling of drought. On the
seaside the surf beats high, flushing, flooding the low
black forelands. On the left side, it is impossible not
to admire the send upward of the whole coast, rising
in a body, broken with the occasional jutting of cliffs,
to the zone of the forests and the clouds, where it
rains all afternoon, and the mists creep down and
draw up, and the black groves loom and vanish in
the margin. Austere and barren is this [illegible
word] track; but full of charm; a vital fragrance
of the ocean and the nameless scent of the tropics
about it always; the air rises with the sun in crystal
vortices, and the distance dizzily twinkles, bright as
a gem; there is no sound but the fine resonant boom
of the striking surges and the soothing rustle of its
subsidence. Every here and there too, you come to an
oasis. Wherever there is a house, the shabby palms
and other trees, spring and singly [illegible word]
sheer out of the rock. We found one gemlike grove
of pineapple and mummy apple, mango and palm,
enclosed with the usual dry stone walls; hard by was
a European waiting the turn of the tide by the margin
of his well; as soon as the sea flowed he might be
able to irrigate with brackish water. We skirted one
cliffy cove, full of bursting surges; if it had not been
for the palms and the architecture of the houses that
stood on the high margin, for the canoes that were
putting out to fish, and the bright dresses (green red
and lilac) of the women that sat about the doors at
work, I might have thought myself in Devonshire.
The children hailed the schoolmaster from wayside

houses with a little chorus of "good morning." With
one little maid, knitting her holoku about her in her
embarrassment so as to define her little body like
tights, we held a long conversation. Will you be at
school tomorrow. Yes, sir. Do you like going to
school? Yes, sir. Do you like bathing? No ma'am.
One little babe, entirely naked, scampered into the
house, and came out again equipped with one corner
of a towel; leaning one hand on the post, and applying her raiment with the other, she stood in the doorway in quite a noble attitude, and watched us by. A
white flag for survey purposes, and a poundmasters
notice on a board, were further marks of civilisation.
A little beyond, we turned a projecting corner and
descended on a long flat of lava; on the landward
side, cliffs made a gradient of an amphitheatre, melting as usual into the gross mountain bulk of the island: over these cliffs, rivers of lava had poured in
half a hundred places, had petrified even as they fell,
and now hung upright like sculptured drapery, the
flutings accentuated with white lichen: here and there
the mouth of a cave was seen half blocked with some
green lianas beckoning in the orifice. On the other
hand, the lava flats reached to the sea, in a long surfy
point. Here was a scattered village, two white
churches, one Protestant, one Catholic, the Catholic
entirely neat, a miserable schoolhouse, and quite a
grove of tall and rather scraggy palms. The whole
sea end of the point was sacred to old days. On the
lava flow, great ramparts from twelve to fifteen feet
in height and of an equal thickness, enclosed two
contiguous quadrilaterals, one large (perhaps an acre
and a half), one smaller. The stones were well set

though without mortar; in parts they were still true
to the plummet; but in the most part of their course
they were partly ruinous from the shock of earthquakes, and the whole sea front has been obliterated
by the surf. Palm trees are scattered all about the
enclosure. Off the point, not a cable's length from the
breach of the sea, rode the schooner that is to cap-
tivate the lepers. This is the Hale o Keawe, the city
of refuge. A dozen natives accompanied us to and
fro, showing us the boundaries and telling us broken
fragments of tradition. The larger quadrilateral was
the city of refuge; the gate was on the seaside and is
now obliterated; the mere entrance was enough, the
guilty person could go forth again safe, so that it
was far more effectual than our European sanctuar-
ies. The smaller is more properly the Hale o Keawe,
whatever that may have been. Where the two join is
a great platform as high as the ramparts: the heiau,
or temple, which you may reconstitute in fancy with
its huge, ungainly, childish idols standing upright on
the margin, and its human victim freshly exposed.
Consider too the manner in which the victim fell;
there may have been a scarcity of proper subjects, and
the priest may have been driven to that most abhorrent practise of the ambuscade, lying in a thicket
uttering lamentable complaints as of a person sick or
injured and when any came to his assistance instantly
dispatching him. What is fabled of the crocodile, was
thus literally true of the reverend gentleman; Marty
Emmet [?] must inspire me: "A damed bad religion" indeed. And yet here, like a flower out of a
dung heap, was the city of safety close beside, the
goal of many a desperate race upon the broken lava.

APPENDIX

—Head of the Heiau, was a great stone, called Kaahumanu (I was told) after Kamehameha's favorite queen. And the tale is worth telling. Kaahumanu, high born, queenly, beautiful lady, the destroyer of tabus, one of the chief friends of Christianity, was in the days of her youth a source of concern to her formidable lord. He bent her with a swivel (whatever that may be) for [the] king said a chief was handsome; and doubtless he knew what he was about; for when he had passed a special enactment decreeing death against any who should commit adultery with her, the lady was so light, and a gentleman by the name of Kanihonui was so complaisant, that the forfeit was actually paid. Nothing of course was done to Kaahumanu. Mr. Bingham says this story draws a fearful picture of the "helpless moral condition" of Hawaii; and I am rejoiced to be able to agree with him for once: it is a singular instance; I cannot hope it should occur again. She was "beautiful *for a Polynesian,*" says he on the same page, testifying to a degree of prejudice that would utterly unfit a man to be a missionary to angels; he thinks all the heathen go to Hell, he testifies it in a hundred places; I will trouble you for the glad tidings! When he and his brethren saw the Polynesians in their own attire—"much of their skins bare," says he, more honest than most missionaries who I am sorry to say continually use the expression naked about people clothed with perfect tropical decency—and again he describes the king as "destitute" think of it! "of hat, gloves, shoes, stockings and pants" an exact description of my own attire in warm weather, and of that of the Tahitians today, and of

197

most Highlanders till yesterday, all quite as decent
people as Bingham. Well, when they saw them, "the
appearance . . . was appalling. Some of our number, with gushing tears, turned away from the spectacle. Others with firmer nerve continued their gaze,
but were ready to exclaim, 'Can these be human beings?'" Even so, O Bingham! and a blessed sight
better these two than you or your excellent spouse
with "the large projecting fore-parts of her bonnet in
the fashion of 1819," which awoke so much mirth
and earned your party a nickname in Hawaii! And
these [illegible word] were the missionaries of civilization and of Christianity, and Bingham was a fine
fellow and had talent, which is the richest of the
joke. Think of me goaded to pick quarrels with this
devoted pioneer of better things. But I trust no one
supposes I would not sooner be Bingham with all
his degrading superstitions, and [two words illegi-
ble] vulgarities in the religious "fashion of 1819,"
than myself in the glories of 1889. The superiority I
claim is that I can see his.—But to return to Kaahumanu. Kamehameha married one of her younger
sisters (he married two of them before he was done)
and my lady fled from court, came to the sanctuary by
sea—swimming, the natives told me—and hid herself
under that great stone which now passes by her name.
Word was brought the king, and a messenger seems
to have recalled the indignant favorite. But here is
another firm instance of how jealousy is a mere question of vanity, unconnected with love or chastity or
any higher feeling; for surely the lady who gave
Kanihonui to the scaffold was not particular in love

affairs, though she had the heart of a lioness, and was in the old days a noble woman.

My dream: say it was a roman villa, and the schooner was a yacht, and we were a great party and one was a lady in a riding habit.

After my two days of riding, I was pitiably stiff, and my hostess shampooed me in the evening. Lomilomi is the Hawaiian word: Taurumi, the Tahitian. And the practice differs even more widely than the names; as squarefaced gin to an agreeable sedative, Lomilomi stands to Taurumi. There are good moments indeed in the first, but a vast deal of harshness, and it has none of the bland soporific influence of its southern congener.

In the speaking in court, I was much struck to compare the language with Tahitian and to find it thicker and harsher. So far as regards l and r, it was what I should have expected, for l, although a beautiful sound, requires discretion, and r is always trustworthy. But I should have here thought T a harsher sound than R; and it is not so: continual R's give a strong thick gutteral quality to the written tongue, while the countless ts of the Tahitian trip off the tongue like crystal.

Wednesday May 2nd [May 1]. In the sun, after the recent grateful rains, Hookena shone out green, under the black lip of the overhanging crag: green as a May orchard in England. The lawn might have been some rich black loam. Even across the steepest slope, the crannied herbs and the clump of prickly pear, carried a flicker of verdure. The air steamed from the baked flats in twisting filaments, like water in a spring, and the further landscape gleamed and trembled through the vortices. In front, a surf too beautiful for language, besieged the foreland; fountains flew in the air; the lava caves hummed and boomed and vomited refluent foam; the flats shone blue with quaking pools; the air was redolent of the ocean: the breeze was the true breeze of the tropics, entrancingly cool, with never a hint of cold. [In the margin, Stevenson has added these words: Bingham talks about the mild sun of Oahu "withering their physical powers."] It was altogether a morning to put one in thought of the antiquity, the health and the cleanness of this earth. And something of that sort was in my mind, when I came in view of the leper house; there was a figure in each of the two doors, on the broken lava at the threshold, a whole family party was seated, women and children in their usual bright attire; in the midst a bowed figure swathed in black; and not far off a horse was hobbled. As I drew nearer I was aware of long drawn lamentable strains of song. It was with none of their new Christian hymns, the work of Taiana or Binamu [Bingham], that figure in the puke Himeni Hawaii [Hawaiian hymnbook, 1823]; but with old Heathen verses, in the old heathen recitative, that they said farewell to their doomed kinsman. [In the margin, Stevenson has added these words: Bingham boasts of the decay of coasting (hoolua [holua] play) as following "the introduction of schools for the elevation of the nation."]

The scene would have killed me when I was younger; today, even with the knowledge that I had myself put my head in the lion's mouth, and might even be carrying the germs of solitude and death in life, I could not but admire the callousness of middle age in my own case; for I saw and heard this horrible and beautiful tragedy with composure. The bowed figure in the midst, I learned subsequently, was the leper herself, a girl of nineteen, already a bad case, her face hugely swollen and "her eyes drawn down," had been two years hiding with her mother in the mountains; and that morning the police got hands on her; she would be put on board the schooner for Molokai, her friends wailing aloud and rolling themselves along the sand; it would carry her to Molokai, and that which I heard was the farewell improvisation of the mother, pouring out her soul in the old Hawaiian manner. "That was not singing," Mrs. Robert corrected me, "that was crying." And she gave me some sketch of what the words would be "O my daughter, O my child, now you are going away from me, now you are taken away from me at last &c." There are still two lepers on the mountain; both armed. The friends supply them not with food alone but ammunition; and it behooves the police to proceed warily when they pursue such invalids. Here, as in Tahiti the natives have no fear of the complaint; the whole family would accompany the stricken one to Molokai, if that were suffered; but strangers, not perhaps from any juster view of hygiene, rather from the tame, law-abiding instinct of the race, will sometimes betray the refuge of a fugitive. Letters, come & go between the exiles and the folk at home (a hundred letters makes the [illegible word] weekly mailbag of Hookena; and it is certain they find Molokai a pleasant place; and look back perhaps with wonder and regret to the days when they were in the forest, and might sing with their own poet:

> . . . In the land of distress,
> My dwelling was on the mountain height,
> My talking companions were the birds,
> The decaying leaves of the ki my clothing
> —Ancient Hawaiian Song.

Friday. When I came up to the pest house, about seven in the morning, there was quite a party present; three or four women as many children, and the policeman. Both doors were open; a fire was burning and a pot cooking on the lava, under the superintendence of an old woman, in a light green dress; she hailed me and offered me her knee to sit on, with a protervity of manner very shocking one of of her age and at such a place and time; so that I had hard ado to call up a smile of refusal. The policeman fetched a chair for me instead, where I sat while he and Amalu seriously consulted. The two sufferers sat in the midst of the group, not even the children to my sorrow avoiding them; the older woman chatting at intervals with a friend, the girl, in the same black weed, bowed in the same attitude as yesterday. It was very plain she would conceal (if possible) her face. Presently I was told nothing was required but money, which (forgetting I was in the South Seas) I would have handed over without more ceremony. The pained expression of Amalu reminded me things must go otherwise. So we stood up together in front of the two patients. I made the due speech, and Amalu translated it sentence by sentence. And when all had been arranged the two women said "Mahalo" with no great expression, the girl not even then displaying her poor face. The policeman followed me to Amalu's with fervent thanks; and that same afternoon requested my leave to put the circumstance in the nupepa [newspaper]: which I chronicle for the idea seems to me kindly on the part of one who lives in so much danger from lepers, and certainly it was delicate to ask.

About nine or ten the schooner lay to outside and a whale boat came ashore. Most of the people of Hookena clustered on the rocks; the first to come was the older leper quite unattended; behind her, after a little, the girl followed, tricked out in a red holoku and with a fine red ribbon in her hat; in this bravery, it was more affecting than ever, to see her move apart on the lava, and crouch in her accustomed attitude. There was a stirring in the crowd, as an older woman perhaps of forty years, still handsome, of a gallant swaggering carriage and a bold, taking countenance (face), drew down on the rocks. I knew at once, without being told, that this was the mother. She came, swinging her hat, rolling her eyes and shoulders to and fro, visibly working herself up. Right in the midst of the group, she sat down, and immediately raised that keen, tremulous wail. As one after another of her friends drew near, she threw out one arm, embraced them down, rolled awhile with them embraced, and then passionately kissed them. The leper girl, at last, as at some signal, rose from her far off place, drew near, was inarmed like the rest, and with a small knot (I suppose of the most intimate) held some while in a general clasp. All this time, the wail continued, rising into words and a sort of passionate, declamatory recitative as each new friend drew near, sinking again, as they rolled together, into the prolonged tremolo. Then one after another, the lepers and the mother were helped into the whale boat; she was gotten under way, ran between the reefs into a bursting surf, and swung next moment without on the smooth swell. I had time to be aware that almost every countenance about me streamed with tears.

Next afternoon we sat waiting in the store for the "Hall," chair brought, center of talk, "the refuse," ancestor worship, comparative religions; ghosts staring a delicious jest to them which shows how far they have travelled from Southern views.

The king in Honaunau. Keawe was a great, ancient chief, to whom Kalakaua himself traces his descent. It was his bones that made the place sacrosanct; and with some cause, since when the tabus were broken, he appeared in a dream first to the keeper's wife, then to the keeper, then to both at once, bidding them arise at once and hide his bones. The last warning roused them; they hastened with a torch into the crypt, exchanged the bones of Keawe with those of another and less holy chieftain; and were back in bed indeed, but not yet asleep, and the sun had not yet risen, when the messengers of Kaahumanu came to demand the precious relics for destruction. The door, according to report, was in the sea-front of the promontory, under water, and must be found by diving. The refuge only protected *victims*. Those of the doomed families, "slaves" they called them, enjoyed a thousand privileges: they were indeed, while the bolt delayed to fall, princes; a slave might have gone abroad in the king's malo [loincloth] even, and gone unpunished; and when the tabu days drew near, they had acquaintance enough in the priests families to get only word of what was doing and lay close in their own houses, where (I gather?) they were safe. But a life of so much danger and privilege turned the head; slaves, even at the dangerous season, went abroad upon their pleasures; they were often caught in the open, and must then run for the Hale o Keawe, with the priestly murderers at their tale.